9/1/89

A delightful collection of M.G. roadsters—gathered for an advertising photograph as the MGB neared the end of its production.

Illustrated **M.G.**

BUYER'S GUIDE™

Richard Knudson

Motorbooks International
Publishers & Wholesalers Inc
Osceola, Wisconsin 54020, USA ®

First published in 1983 by Motorbooks International Publishers & Wholesalers Inc, P O Box 2, 729 Prospect Avenue, Osceola, WI 54020 USA

Printed and bound in the United States of America

The information in this book is true and complete to the best of our knowledge. All recommendations are made without any guarantee on the part of the author or publisher, who also disclaim any liability incurred in connection with the use of this data or specific details.

We recognize that some words, model names and designations, for example, mentioned herein are the property of the trademark owner. We use them for identification purposes only. This is not an official publication

Library of Congress Cataloging in Publication Data

Knudson, Richard L.
  Illustrated M.G. buyer's guide.

  1. M.G. automobile—Purchasing. 2. M.G. automobile—Collectors and collecting. I. Title. II. Title: Illustrated MG buyer's guide.
  TL215.M2K57   1983 629.2'222   82-20867
  ISBN 0-87938-169-8 (soft)

On the front cover: Gregg Brandow's 1967 MGB, slightly modified to taste, courtesy of Quality Coaches. *Michael Dregni*
On the back cover: The Inskip four-seater TD. *Dave Jensen*

Motorbooks International books are also available at discounts in bulk quantity for industrial or sales-promotional use. For details write to Special Sales Manager at the Publisher's address

The publisher wishes to acknowledge its gratitude to
Mr. Windom L. Estes, Mr. Chris Nowlan and Mr. Bob Stone
for their contributions to the MGA, MGB and MGC chapters.
Also thanks to Mr. John Blunsden of Motor Racing
Publications for his photographic contributions.

PREFACE

I suppose that M.G. has been as logical as any other manufacturer in its model designations. Using letters for the most part, it really hasn't been too confusing. Looked at in total, M.G. really does have a most impressive production record.

Much of M.G.'s success as a producer of a sports car with an excellent reputation was the result of a dedicated work force. It might sound like hype from a public relations person to say that the average M.G. worker was more dedicated *and* happier than his counterpart at other British factories, but it's true. A look at the work record shows that M.G. lost fewer days to strikes and other labor problems than anyone else in the industry. There was an Abingdon spirit. It remains to be seen if the M.G. Metro continues in it.

TABLE OF CONTENTS

INTRODUCTION

Cheap and cheerful! If that never was an M.G. advertising slogan, it should have been.

That's what Cecil Kimber had in mind when the first M.G. Midget appeared in 1929. He knew that not only rich people wanted a sports car but also that everyone who enjoyed motoring wanted one as well. So the M-Type Midget was born and the tradition of an inexpensive, mass-produced sports car started in the Thames town of Abingdon in England. Kimber was to sports cars what Ford was to mass-produced cars: Kimber offered the sports car to the working man while Ford put the passenger car within the reach of his workers. The idea that a sports car could be financially possible for the average person was unique in 1929.

But price wasn't the only appeal for the Midget. It was an honest and straightforward little car that was as easy to work on as it was eager to perform. And perform it did; few sports cars can claim the competition breeding that M.G. experienced in the nineteen thirties.

For the vintage car enthusiast, the racing history probably isn't as important as the simplicity of restoration and maintenance of the car. That one characteristic makes M.G. a very attractive collector automobile today. Owning a vintage M.G. does not require a full-time mechanic. Given some basic mechanical sense, good tools, a manual and true desire, anyone should be able to keep an M.G. on the road.

Okay. You like vintage sports cars and you have decided to shop for an M.G. What steps should you take? Well, you've done the first thing right: You bought this book. Read it carefully. Note particularly the references to further reading at the end of the book. Do try to read those articles and/or books mentioned and they will help you before and after your purchase.

You will also find a reference to clubs that cater to the models discussed with complete addresses at the end of the book. Join the club and/or register that specializes in the model you're interested in; you'll find that the newsletter or magazine you'll receive will be of great benefit. You will also make contacts for the purchase of a car as well as subsequent advice.

After you have purchased a car, go to one of the club's major meetings *before* you begin your restoration. You need to know what the potential of your car really is, and a big meet is the only place to find out. In addition, you'll wind up in the company of people who feel the same way about their cars as you do about yours.

For Americans it used to be cheaper to go to England to buy an old M.G., but that no longer seems to be the case. In fact, the British are coming over to the North American side of the Atlantic to find post-World War II M.G.'s to take back to the homeland. Because very few pre-1940 M.G.'s were exported, these cars are more difficult to find in the US and Canada. If your heart is set on an MMM car (Midget, Magna, Magnette—the overhead cam cars), then the best place to look is England. But, regardless of where you live, do not, under any circumstances, make your deal by mail. Great as the ads sound, you must see the car for yourself. So be prepared to spend the extra money for the trip. You'll be glad you did.

The first concern when viewing an unrestored car should be its completeness. Is everything there? What's missing? Are the missing bits available? How expensive are they? Happily, there are several reliable parts suppliers, all of whom produce illustrated catalogs. Be sure to have at least one of these catalogs with you when shopping for a car. That way you'll know what the missing parts will cost. You'll also let the seller know that you are a person to reckon with.

Old Number One is the first purebred sports car to be known as an M.G. There were earlier specials, but this was the first designed as a sports car. Author photo.

The major vintage M.G. parts suppliers deserve a bit of praise here. They really are doing the M.G. enthusiast a great service by not only finding new old stock (NOS) parts, but also by manufacturing needed replacement parts. Often they remanufacture slow-moving parts because the part is necessary to complete a restoration. This shows an admirable concern for the hobby, and they are to be commended for it.

When buying a pre-MGA car, one is apt to be offered two alternatives. Either the car is an "older" restoration or it is a car in need of complete restoration—perhaps a "basket case."

Let's consider the "older" restoration first. For example, the car was restored five years earlier and has 12,000 miles since the restoration. It probably looks fine and runs well; beauty, however, is often only fresh-wax-deep. You can check to see if the restoration is holding up so that you'll be able to enjoy the car for several years before having to do it again. The owner will probably tell you it was a frame up restoration. This means the body came off the frame. Ask about the wood: How much of it was replaced? The bodies of earlier M.G. models have an ash frame over which the sheet metal is fitted. This wood is subject to rot and failure. Being a shrewd buyer, you must also check the *condition* of the wood. There will be a major sill on each side of the car that is particularly vulnerable to rot. It can be easily seen (the running board bolts go through it) and tested with an awl: If the sill can be punctured easily, then it is rotten.

The front and rear door posts are also weak points on these wood-framed cars. How do the doors fit? Is the striker plate loose? Are the hinges solidly attached to the post (hinge pins wear, and they may allow door movement when open—this, in itself, is not a serious problem)?

The other major spot for wood rot is in the large piece of plywood under the gasoline tank. One can test this with an awl from inside the side curtain compartment. While plywood is more prone to water damage than ash, rot here *probably* means that the rest of the timber frame is suspect.

If you are planning to drive this "older" restoration for a few years, then it should be pleasing to your eye. Is the paint in good shape? Can it be matched? How about the chrome? Was it redone? Is there any flaking? If the car has bumpers, these should be straight and free of dents and peeled chrome. The grille shell and windscreen frame are extremely visible and the chrome should be good on both. Headlamp shells are apt to be dented by clumsy or careless hood handling. Repair to these is possible but costly.

The interior, top and side curtains should be in good shape if the car has been restored. If any of these areas are terribly tatty, then be suspicious of the car really being an "older" restoration.

A careful look at the engine compartment can reveal a great deal about an automobile and the care it has had. First, is the engine the original one belonging to that car? Check the numbers on the block and on the maker's plate to be *reasonably* sure (it is possible to replace the tag on the block to match the maker's plate). Even more important to the ultimate value of the car is to be absolutely sure that the engine is the correct type for the car; for instance, a TD must have an XPAG/TD engine in it. Fitting an engine from, say, an MGB would decrease the value of the car as much as if it had a Ford V-8 in it.

Next, use your reference books to ensure that the engine is as near original looking as possible. Does it have the correct air cleaners? Are the rocker cover and side plate proper?

Cleanliness can say a great deal (if the engine wasn't just steam cleaned). Some wag once said that the only way to cure an M.G. engine's oil leak is to run it without oil. Well, it's not quite that desperate; there will be some oil present, but it certainly should not be all over the place. Run the car until it's at operating temperature (70°C), then start looking for oil leaks in earnest: Check the rocker cover and side plate. Then, to put the owner off guard, with the engine running spread some newsprint on the ground under the engine and transmission—any serious oil leak will show like footprints in fresh concrete.

The firewall can also reveal quite a bit. The wires should be fresh-looking and the colors should be clear. Extra wires just should not exist.

All right, how does it run? At operating temperature, the oil pressure should be within the limits stated in the appropriate manual. Check the compression as well. Smoke from the exhaust is not normal. The engine should start quickly and run smoothly. When driving the car, performance should be brisk if not neck-snapping.

The transmission on virtually every model M.G. is easy to use. Certain prewar cars had nonsynchro boxes, but easy gear changing has been an M.G. hallmark. Assuming you know how to shift gears on that particular car, the transmission should be trouble free. Grinding noises, howling, rattles and jumping out of gear are all signs of trouble—the older the car, the more expensive the repair (usually).

While the major details for examining a pre-MGA car for potential purchase also apply to the later cars, the more modern ones replace the earlier wood problems with something worse—rust. Although the MGA does have a separate chassis, it is every bit as susceptible to rust as are all of the unibody M.G.'s produced during the post-1955 years. Look for rust problems in the rocker panels, under the fenders and in the trunk. Rust can be fixed, but it isn't easy.

Given the interest and just a bit of skill, any owner should be able to do much of the restoration at home. The cars are just not complicated. Considering the world's economy today, one would have to be wealthy to have the car done at a professional shop. The hourly rate at a shop is the same regardless if the work is being done on a TC or a Rolls Royce. The restoration costs on the two cars would be about the same, but the end values of the two cars would be far apart even though the investment might be the same.

Let's try to break the costs down further by looking at a hypothetical car: a T Series roadster offered at $25,000. The car is an obvious show winner and has a trophy or two to prove it. Is it really worth $25,000? We have to assume that this is a body off, frame up restoration—no doubt the owner has the photos and bills to prove it. This is probably the way he'd justify the price (remember, these prices are relative and based on current costs and the asking price):

1.	original unrestored car	$6,000
2.	chassis restoration	1,500
3.	wheels and tires	1,000
4.	engine and transmission	3,500
5.	rear end	200
6.	chrome	1,000
7.	body and paint	5,500
8.	interior and top	1,800
	Total Investment	$21,000

1. The price of the unrestored car is always the big question mark. Sometimes real bargains turn up, but the opposite usually is the case. The cheaper the car can be obtained, the easier it is to splurge on various aspects of the restoration.

2. By doing it yourself, one could cut this way down. Going all the way here means dipping the chassis, replacing virtually all parts and then having it sprayed with one of the new epoxy-based paints. By doing it yourself with a paint scraper and wire brush, replacing only worn parts, and painting it with spray cans, the end result (with care) might not be all that different. It depends, really, on what your ultimate goal is: Do you want a show stopper or merely a beautiful car to enjoy?

3. Every car needs wheels and tires. Splurges here might include chromed wire wheels; but outside of that, it's tough to save money on these items. Wheels have to be trued and painted, and tires should be new. One can save some money on the larger tires by going to a nonoriginal brand name.

4. Saving money on the engine and transmission means doing it yourself plus having some luck. By following the manual, disassembly and assembly are not too difficult. Once apart, the engine and most of its parts will have to go to a reliable machine shop for some work. The parts will be thoroughly cleaned (boiled). The machinists will check the cylinder bore and determine if the block needs boring; if it does, they will need the new pistons before the boring is done. The rods and crank will be magnafluxed—if you're lucky, there will be no cracks. (If cracks appear in the magnafluxing, you are in for a major expense.) The rest of the engine and transmission work includes examining carefully every part and replacing those that are worn. Do-it-yourselfers save labor time, but engine and transmission parts are very expensive. Merely replacing rings and bearings is no way to do it and will undoubtedly be more expensive in the end. If someone says that he spent $3,500 on the engine and transmission, believe it.

5. Generally, M.G. rear ends are very dependable. Replacing bearings and seals is a must. If you're going to be driving the car, then new half-shafts should be considered.

6. Chrome work is expensive. Recommending a chromer is like recommending a restaurant: One can never guarantee the results. It's best to find one you like, and stay with him. If you choose to have everything done, then it is not very hard to spend $1,000. I have a personal preference for keeping as many original parts on a car as possible rather than replacing something just because a new replacement or reproduction is available. I like the looks of old chrome on some parts—but, then, I don't win concours trophies.

7. Bodywork and painting are the most difficult for the home restorer. Most home shops don't have, for instance, an air compressor that can produce a first-class paint job. The owner can, however, do much of the preparation and the wood repair before the body tub goes in for the final painting. The choice of painter and the ultimate finish will determine the total cost. It could amount to as much as twenty-five percent of the total value of the car; or as little as five percent. It is interesting that the difference between a $1,000 paint job and a $5,000 paint job to the untrained eye might not be discernible.

8. For most models there are great replacement tops and interior kits available. For an outstanding job, one should have them professionally installed, but it is not impossible to do a very acceptable job at home.

This analysis shows that most asking prices for genuinely restored M.G.'s are not terribly out of line. It also proves that by doing much of the work yourself, you can save money. By working on your car, you'll develop a respect for it and be on your way to being an enthusiast rather than a mere owner. The M.G. hobby is full of nice people who enjoy their cars. Enthusiasm has always been a prerequisite for owning an M.G. Other famous marques require money first, and the loyalty might follow. Not so with the cheap and cheerful M.G.— let's keep it that way!

Richard Knudson
July 1983

INVESTMENT RATING

★★★★★ These are rare cars which command very high prices. Don't be fooled because many of the cars with this rating are actively raced by their owners: M.G.'s inspire that sort of use. Since there aren't many of these cars, the prices will probably hold. Once in awhile one will come up at auction, but usually they change hands very quietly. Unbelievable as it may seem, one has to be very careful of replicas and blatant fakes.

★★★★ The most desirable M.G.'s of the obtainable models. Since they are sought after, the prices are high and will stay that way. At this writing prices seem to have topped out, but an upswing of the economy could change that. There just aren't all that many M.G.'s in this class available so a sudden drop in the economy probably would not cause values to drop on these cars.

★★★ The sleepers in the M.G. hobby. These cars have all of the attributes which made M.G. famous, yet they have not really caught on with the enthusiasts at this writing.

★★ Driving M.G.'s has always been fun, and these cars fill that desire very well. Cars in this class will aways be enjoyable even though they probably won't ever be rapidly (or even moderately) appreciating investment cars.

CHAPTER 1
THE OVERHEAD CAM MIDGETS

Convinced that the public was ready for an affordable sports car, Cecil Kimber introduced the M Type Midget in 1928. The M Type was simple, inexpensive and competitive in motor sport. Those three principles eventually made M.G. the world's leading producer of sports cars.

Morris Motors Limited introduced a small economy car called the Morris Minor in the late summer of 1928. M.G. was doing all right with its six-cylinder models, but Kimber had that vision of a sports car for everyone. When the tiny Minor appeared, he acted. The result was the M Type Midget, which was *introduced* at the fall motor show in London. Yes, that was fast work, but the chassis and the engine were very suitable.

The bodies of the earlier M Types had the traditional ash frame but were covered in fabric. As fragile as it may sound, this was really an extremely good arrangement. Think of it: no dents, just a few rips and tears to patch once in awhile. Later versions were covered with sheet metal. Today, restorers can easily find reproduction bodies with either covering at reasonable prices. The convenience of being able to obtain new bodies is making it easier to make fake M Types. There were an awful lot of those Minors around, you know. The possibility of being offered a fake means you should know your seller *and* check chassis numbers.

The most fragile part of the M Type was the crankshaft. Since it was only supported by two main bearings, and since drivers tended to over-rev the little 847 cc engine in search of more speed, that crankshaft could snap as easily as a teenager's bubble gum.

Driven wisely, the M Type was dependable and a great little competitor. It was the basis of some great M.G. record cars as well as race cars that came later.

The engine of all the Midgets in this chapter had the overhead camshaft which was technically extremely interesting. The camshaft was gear-driven by the armature shaft of the vertically mounted generator. You know how much oil is required in the top end of an engine, don't you? Well, that oil had to get back to the crankcase, and many luckless (and lightless) owners figured it all went *through* the generator. That may have been the *first* M.G. oil leak, but I doubt it.

The M Type was also offered in a GT version called the sportsman's coupe. It was certainly "cute" and lived up to the true GT's distinction of having a worthless back seat.

The M Type was first; for that reason, it has good investment potential. M.G.'s of this vintage are much more valuable in England than they are in North America. Perhaps if there are bargains to be found, they will exist in the US and Canada. One must remember, however, that very few cars were exported.

A contemporary of the M Type Midget was the D Type. It was an ugly four-seater—a concept that M.G. persisted in trying to adapt on several models in the early thirties without success. The D Type failed after 250 had been built. To its credit, the D Type utilized some of the knowledge gained from the C Type competition cars. Not many D Types survive, and I doubt if many change hands. With prettier M.G.'s available, why bother?

★★★★ M Type Midget
1928-1932

★★★ D Type Midget
1931-1932

★★★ J1 Midget
1932-1933

★★★★ J2 Midget
1932-1934

★★★★ PA Midget
1934-1935

★★★★ PB Midget
1935-1936

This is the M Type Double Twelve racing model. Author photo.

The J1 and J2 replaced the M Type and D Type in 1932. One can say the same things about the J1 as were said about the D Type. It was an unsuccessful car available as an open four-seater or as a closed salonette. Only 380 of these overweight and underpowered vehicles made it off the line at Abingdon. Collectable? Sure. Investment? Doubtful.

Ah, but the J2 Midget was different. Here was the M.G. styling trend setter. The J2 was an important car. In spite of its chalkstick-like crankshaft engine with only two main bearings, the J2 offered performance and handsome style for a modest price. This is a historical M.G. which is essential to any collection.

The J2 was first offered with cycle fenders before the later version was equipped with the graceful full fenders associated with the TC. More cycle-fendered versions were made than the full-fendered cars, and many full fenders were converted to cycle fenders by boy racers. Since fewer full-fendered cars survive, one would think that these would be the most desirable. Wrong. It seems that more of the boy racer syndrome is present in collectors than might be thought. Good. That means the cars will get used. Anyway, you just might find a full-fendered J2 for less than the sportier cycle-fendered car. In all fairness, it should be pointed out that replacement cycle fenders are much less expensive for the restorer than are full fenders.

In a way, the P Type had it all: delightful early style and a new overhead cam engine with three (count 'em) main bearings. This rugged engine was very reliable and proved to be highly successful when tuned for use in the remarkable Q and R race cars.

An open four-seater was tried but was no more successful than on the D and J. What did succeed, however, was the most beautiful Airline coupe built by Allingham, a London coachbuilder. The most desirable prewar Midget today has to be one with an Airline body.

The Airlines rarely change hands today. A completely restored example would probably be worth what some of the racing M.G.'s bring. The combination of beauty, elegance and rarity would make an Airline a super M.G. investment.

As noted at the beginning of this chapter there were 2,000 PA's built and only 526 PB's. Scarcity alone might give the PB a slight edge for investment potential. The PB had a 939 cc engine compared to the PA's 847 cc unit—that amounted to 43.3 horsepower for the PB and 34.9 for the PA.

Parts are not a major problem for these overhead cam Midgets. Many reproduction parts are available (mostly from England). If anything, these Midgets are easier to restore than the postwar T Types. If you're buying a classic sports car to use on long trips, then those examples with only two main bearings should certainly be avoided. Other than that, it's a matter of personal taste and availability.

Prices for any of these Midgets should be in the TC range. Bare chassis are often available, and used parts are often offered. When buying used parts in any quantity, one should always make the journey to inspect and collect. I have heard many horror stories of people buying parts by mail and being sent a pile of rubbish in return for their cash. No, for fifty-year-old used auto parts, you must be prepared to go and look at them.

These early Midgets may make better investments for another reason: Once restored, owners are apt not to use them the way they might use a later car. The restoration, then, will last longer; thus the investment is better protected. I won't discuss the philosophy of whether it's more enjoyable to look at a car or drive it—that subject is better left to the club journals. One thing remains: These overhead cam Midgets are steeped in M.G. lore, and are true sports cars to be savored forever.

M Type Sportsman's Coupe: the first M.G. GT?
British Leyland photo.

M Type Midget. British Leyland photo.

Two M Types: Double Twelve (SC9559) and the normal version
(MG787). Author photo.

D Type prototype. British Leyland photo.

Two heavy adults in the rear of the diminutive D Type could really change the handling characteristics and make the steering very light. British Leyland photo.

J1 four-seater. British Leyland photo.

A swept-wing J2 from the front. Author photo.

A swept-wing J2. British Leyland photo.

MODEL	YEARS PRODUCED	TOTAL BUILT	CYLINDERS	DISPLACEMENT (cc's)	WHEELBASE	HORSEPOWER
M	1928-1932	3,235	4	847	6' 6" 7' and	20-27
D	1931-1932	250	4	847	7' 2"	27
J1	1932-1933	380	4	847	7' 2"	36
J2	1932-1934	2,083	4	847	7' 2"	36
PA	1934-1935	2,000				
PB	1935-1936	526				

A cycle-wing J2 Midget with full weather production. British Leyland photo.

P Type four-seater from the rear. Author photo.

P Type four-seater. British Leyland photo.

The P Type two-seater from above and the front. British Leyland
photos.

The beautiful P Type Airline coupe, probably the most handsome coupe M.G. ever produced. British Leyland photo.

CHAPTER 2

MAGNAS AND MAGNETTES

While M.G.'s are commonly thought of as four-cylinder cars, their six-cylinder tradition is solid if not so well known. The first six-cylinder M.G. was the 18/80 which was introduced in 1928 and the last was the MGC of 1967-69. The foundation of this six-cylinder tradition rests with the Magnas and the Magnettes produced between 1931 and 1936.

First was the F Type Magna. With a production run of 1,250, it was the most popular. The C Type chassis was stretched ten inches to seven feet ten inches, and two cylinders were added to the M Type's four. This six produced only some thirty-seven horsepower and the performance was less than startling. But the F Type was a genuine sports car that looked the part. It must have been the right car for the time because it sold well.

The F Type in any of its various body styles was very nice looking. Maybe that's why it enjoyed good sales. It was offered in the following body styles: four-seat open, four-seat salonette, two-seat open. The car was also popular with various English coachbuilders, and some nice special-bodied cars were built by them.

All of the F Types had a great four-speed gearbox that proved to be popular with racing car builders. The later F Types had twelve-inch brakes. All in all, the F Type is a most acceptable classic M.G.

The mere mention of a K Type can cause even a seasoned M.G. enthusiast's eyes to glaze over. But he'll be thinking of the likes of Eyston, Nuvolari and Hall rather than the more mundane production K Types that begot the famous K3.

One of the major changes for the K Type was a new engine. The displacement was a mere 1087 cc (not much when you consider that, today, several motorcycles have more). Power was up, but not by much. Some models were fitted with a preselector transmission. With this interesting gearbox, the driver selected a gear by moving the lever, then, when needed, he depressed the clutch and the change was made. For instance, say you see a turn coming up. First, select third on the lever. Then, with both hands on the steering wheel, enter the turn. When you want third to accelerate out of the turn, merely stab the clutch and it's done. Very neat and safe.

The K Magnettes were offered in several versions, each a bit different from the others. There were three different chassis: K1, K2 and K3. And there were four different engines: KA, KB, KD and K3. (The K3 was a racing car and is covered elsewhere in this book.) To complicate matters there were four different body choices: four-seat saloon, four-seat tourer, four-seat open and two-seat open.

Of all the body styles, I think the pillarless saloon is the most attractive from a collector's standpoint. The concept of a four-door car without a center post to close on is unique even today. Ralph Nader would be quick to find fault with having no center roof support—thank goodness he wasn't around in the thirties.

The only clear explanation of the K Type mysteries and confusing designations is in *MG by McComb* (pp 93-96). But even after a careful reading, I'd hate to have to pass a test on it.

★★★★ **F Type Magna**
1931-1932
★★★★ **K Type Magnette**
1932-1934
★★★★ **L Type Magna**
1933-1934
★★★★ **NA Magnette**
1934-1936
★★★★ **KN Magnette**
1934-1935

F Type salonette. Ron Cover photo.

The L Type Magna appeared in most of the same body styles as the other Magnas and Magnettes with the exception of the Continental coupe. The Continental coupe proved unpopular at the time of its production. Since few were made, and since it was unique, it is a very desirable model today.

At a quick glance, the L Magna two-seater looks like a large J2. All of the L's had swept fenders in contrast with the cycle wings on the F's. A few more horses were squeezed out of the 1087 cc engine, and the result was a nice-looking car that went well. This is an excellent vintage M.G. to own.

The last of these Magnas and Magnettes was the N, and it was the best of the lot. It may have been good because the design engineers focused their attention on it. Whatever the reason, the end result was an excellent motor car.

The engine was a robust 1271 cc that produced 56 bhp. It could really push these cars along at very fast rates of speed. In all versions, the body styling was very sophisticated. The customer could easily see that he was getting much more than a stretched Midget. Body styles offered included two-seat open, four-seat open and the handsome Airline coupe.

N Types were highly successful on the road as well as in competition. Several were converted to single-seaters for racing at Brooklands and at other events. The N also had a racing version, the NE Magnette, which is discussed in another chapter.

Sagging sales left the works with several extra saloon bodies and K chassis. It was decided to fit the N Type 1271 cc engine and call the car the KN. It sold quite well and cleared up those unused parts.

All of these Magnas and Magnettes are extremely collectable today. What made them popular or unpopular in the early thirties is of little consequence today. Now, they are equally collectable and restorable. Each is worth pretty much the same as another. The notable examples of high-priced models would be the K pillarless saloon, the L Continental coupe and the N Airline coupe. The other two- and four-seaters would be about the same value regardless of the type represented.

Unrestored examples of these automobiles keep appearing. They are well worth buying and restoring as they represent outstanding vintage motoring.

F Type salonette. British Leyland photo.

F Type two-seater. British Leyland photo.

A K Type two-seater. Wiard Krook photo.

Two views of the K Type pillarless saloon. Author and British Leyland photos.

The ash body frame for the pillarless saloon. Most pre-MGA M.G.'s carried bodies that featured a wood frame under a steel skin. British Leyland photo.

The N Type served as a basis for many single-seat race cars during the thirties. Author photo.

NA Magnette; front and rear. Ron Cover and British Leyland photos.

MODEL	YEARS PRODUCED	TOTAL BUILT	CYLINDERS	DISPLACE-MENT (cc's)	WHEEL-BASE	HORSE-POWER
F	1931-1932	1,250	6	1271	7' 10"	37.2
				1087	9'	38.8-
K	1932-1934	About 170	6	1271	7' 10 3/16"	54.5
L	1933-1934	576	6	1087	7' 10 3/16"	41
NA	1934-1936	738	6	1271	8'	56.6
KN	1934-1935	201				

NA Magnette being raced. Author photo.

NB Magnette—note the front hinged doors. British Leyland photo.

Worldwide, the best known of all the classic M.G.'s is the T Series. To the uninitiated, M.G. only made the TC, and all M.G.'s are TC's to them.

Well, there is a resemblance. In fact, all M.G.'s from the 1932 J2 through the 1955 TF have styling characteristics which have identified M.G.'s until the present day. Up front is that distinctive square radiator ahead of a long hood. In front of the driver and passenger are two wind-deflecting humps on the cowl. The doors are cut away to provide a comfortable armrest as well as sporting lines. And the rear is as distinctive as any starlet's. The spare tire rests behind a big slab fuel tank. Add it all together, and it says "M.G." and "sports car" to the entire world. This distinctive styling reached its height in the twenty-year reign of the T Series.

TA

In 1935 the M.G. Car Company (formed in 1928) lost most of its independence when it unceremoniously became a part of Nuffield Group. Up to that time, M.G. at Abingdon had operated more or less on its own. With the Morris take-over, however, there were some drastic changes made: Racing was banned, the design office was moved from Abingdon to Cowley, and all branches of Britain's largest auto maker were told to make a profit.

Although the TA was the first Midget designed at Cowley, there was still the Abingdon influence of Cecil Kimber and Syd Enever that persisted over the ensuing years. Enever was a brilliant practical engineer who learned by doing. He was kept at Abingdon to act as a liaison person between the drawing office at Cowley (about ten miles away) and the factory. You can bet that Kimber and Enever fought for M.G. in every instance.

The TA Midget proved to be quite different from previous Midgets. Some of these changes were caused by evolving design improvements while others were motivated by the make money edict.

The car looked about the same as a PB, but it was longer and wider. It possessed good handling and a somewhat softer ride than previous models. Larger coachwork plus more comfort plus a modest price all added up to a car built to sell.

The major change was in the engine compartment. Gone was the familiar overhead camshaft powerplant; in its place was a simple overhead valve engine. This simplicity meant lower production costs and easier owner maintenance.

While the engine change was important to the car's economic success, enthusiasts were sorry to see the gutsy ohc engines cast aside. With the passage of time, we have come to realize that the TA's engine is its weakest part—the cylinder head is prone to cracking. As can be imagined, there is not an endless supply of TA cylinder heads out there, so more and more TA's are winding up with nonoriginal engines in them.

With any car of collector value it is essential that it have the original engine in order to be regarded as a top investment item. The next best thing is having an original *type* engine in it. The third choice, but much less desirable, would be an engine from the same manufacturer (this is often the case with the TA as many have the later XPAG unit installed). A TA with a non-M.G. engine in it would not be worth much to a collector.

★★★ TA

June 1936-April 1939
Chassis Numbers TA0251-TA3253
Engine Numbers MPJG 501-MPJG 3503

★★★ TB

May 1939-September 1939
Chassis Numbers TB0251-TB0629
Engine Numbers XPAG502-XPAG882

★★★★ TC

November 1945-December 1949
Chassis Numbers TC0251-TC10252
Engine Numbers XPAG/TC/833-XPAG/TC/10835

★★★★ TD

November 1949-September 1953
Chassis Numbers TD0251-TD29915
Engine Numbers XPAG/TD/501-XPAG/TD/30300

★★★★ TF

October 1953-May 1955
TF 1250 Chassis Numbers 0501-6500, 6651-6750, 6851-6950
TF 1500 Chassis Numbers 6501-6650, 6751-6850, 6951-10100
TF 1250 Engine Numbers XPAG/TF/30303-XPAG/TF/36516
TF 1500 Engine Numbers XPEG 501-XPEG 3940

TA Midget was the first of the T Series. British Leyland photo.

There were two alternative body styles that are great favorites of collectors: the Tickford and the Airline coupe. The Tickford is a luxurious car that featured wind-up windows as well as a three-position top. The Tickford is a gorgeous car and is most desirable. While over 100 Tickfords were produced, only one TA Airline coupe was supposed to have been built. The Airline coupe was an extremely popular body on earlier M.G.'s, and its beauty on the TA chassis is every bit as successful. The TA Airline coupe must, of course, be regarded as a museum piece, but TA Tickfords do turn up and are usually priced competitively with TC's.

TA's do not seem to have commanded the prices that the postwar T Series cars command. It may be the reputation of the engine, or the notion that prewar cars are more difficult. Nevertheless, they are bound to appreciate over the years and are every bit as handsome as the TC's.

Driving a TA is just about the same as driving a TB or a TC. One has to pay attention at all times because the steering is very sensitive. Properly maintained, the steering is precise if unforgiving. If any part of the steering mechanism is allowed to get out of adjustment or is improperly lubricated, then the car becomes very tricky to drive. Other than that, the TA behaves exactly as a vintage sports car should: It tracks straight and sticks in the corners. What more could one ask?

The basic problems of the TA's engine brought about a new engine and model some three years later in 1939. The new XPAG unit was adapted from the Morris 10. It was strong and powered about 50,000 new M.G.'s through 1955.

The change to the XPAG engine created a delightful car. Gone were the clutch and cylinder head problems of the MPJG engine; in their place was a powerplant that became noted for its dependability and performance. The transmission used for the TB was the same as that used in the later TC. It was a gearbox that proved to be virtually indestructible.

Amazingly, TB prices, like those of the TA, do not match the postwar cars. In this case, it's not the engine. It may be that since there are so few available, one really can't be sure of the TB market; however, those that do change hands seem to be priced under a TC, TD or TF.

A few TB Tickfords have survived and they are very valuable. By its nature, the Tickford body is much more complicated than the normal TB body. For that reason, it costs up to three times as much to restore; thus, a fully restored TA or TB Tickford would be quite expensive; perhaps twice the cost of a TC.

Again, the TB is as handsome as a TC and its rarity means that it will grow in value each year.

TC

One of the nine cars originally selected for the Milestone Car Society was the M.G. TC. It was selected by the membership of the society as one of its first certified milestones. The oldest of the first group, it was nominated on the strength of its design and performance. Other considerations for certification by the society include: engineering, quality of construction and innovation. When one considers the five categories in total, then it can be easily seen that the TC belonged. Design and performance are essential to a successful sports car, and the TC just may be one of the most successful sports cars ever built when all aspects of that success are considered.

Aesthetically speaking, the TC was and still is a delight to behold. While not unique to the TC model, the big, bold radiator and the long hood leading to it are very striking. Next, the delicate clamshell fenders framing the spidery, nineteen-inch wire wheels complete the picture of a classic sports car. Even with the windscreen erected and all of the weather equipment in place, the automobile looks correct. John Thornley called the K3 the epitome of the

TA Tickford Drophead Coupe. This is one of the prettiest body styles offered before World War II. British Leyland photo.

The TB is the rarest of the T Types. British Leyland photo.

M.G.; he is right when considering the racing M.G.'s, but for the sports cars, the TC comes as near to the epitome as any. A TC was chosen as one of eight automobiles for the New York Museum of Modern Art's exhibit of classic design in 1951. There is no question that the TC is an almost perfect combination of classic look and modern performance.

Today, as ever, there is much discussion regarding the classic look especially among automobile enthusiasts. Whenever the discussion centers on sports cars, the TC is always included. The July 1975 issue of *Road & Track* had a feature article about a special show devoted to the automobile as an art form. It was sponsored by The Newport Harbor Art Museum Council and The Junior League of Newport Harbor and was held at the Newport Beach Marriott in California. This April 1975 show focused on cars which were outstanding combinations of the aesthetic art of the body designer and the technical innovations of the mechanical engineer. The end result was an emphasis on the automobile as a visual art form as it developed since its inception.

The oldest car in the show was a 1903 Autocar; the newest was a 1975 Scirocco coupe. In between were fifty-eight cars which represented a wide variety of marques and which would be readily accepted at any concours in the world. One of the first postwar cars at the show was a 1948 TC. The judges offered the following reasons for including it in the show.

> Things come together with honesty, clarity, delicacy. The overall balance from any view is so digestible and believable. The major impact: fun, excitement, affordability. A classical statement of "dignity" in its smallest automotive form.
> Abingdon's pride won world popularity with its meticulously formed fenders, geometric hood, and neat body.

These words from Harry Bradley, Tom Kellogg and Strother MacMinn appeared in the show's lovely catalog and certainly summarize the feelings knowledgeable enthusiasts have for this delightful sports car from the banks of the Thames.

That the TC was America's first introduction to sports cars is an indisputable fact. True, sports cars and road racing existed in the US prior to World War II; but that was really for a very few exceptional men who were members of the Automobile Racing Club of America. The average American enthusiast was not economically able to think about owning a sports car until after the war. England was flooded with American soldiers at that time, and they were introduced to sports cars which gave amazing performance on twisting country roads even using the low-quality gasoline available then. Many of these cars were M.G.'s. Given the basic American love of the automobile, it should come as no surprise that many GI's brought M.G.'s home when they returned from the war.

And America loved the TC. This handsome car inspired a change in automotive design that is present today: Bucket seats and gear-change levers on the floor (again!) are really a result of the sports car revolution which the TC inspired in North America. We know that the influence of that revolution is still being felt.

Automobile enthusiasts came to know about handling from the TC. The road test cliche "cornering as if on rails" could easily have been coined about the TC. In their book on the M.G., John Christy and Karl Ludvigsen referred to it as a "coffin riding on four harps" which characterizes the TC's square shape and semi-elliptic springs with those delicate nineteen-inch wire wheels on all four corners—not a bad image at all.

For all its beauty, the TC is not fragile. It's as rugged today as ever and can certainly keep up with modern traffic. Of all the T Types, the TC consistently commands the highest prices and most attention. It is a car that will hold its value. And all optimists should remember that with 10,000 of them made, there have to be a few undiscovered ones remaining. Happy looking!

The swept-wing J2 in the foreground is considerably smaller than the TC behind it. Author photo.

TD

The production run of TD's surpassed the entire previous M.G. model output. Simply put, the TD was the most popular M.G. produced through 1952. Like all M.G.'s since, it was the most popular sports car of its time.

If the TC started the sports car revolution, it was the TD that fought the battle. It refined the sports car concept by softening the ride a bit and making it easier to steer while retaining those classic M.G. looks.

The birth of the TD is a typical Abingdon success story. Syd Enever, the brilliant, practical engineer in charge of the development shop was instructed to come up with a replacement for the cart-sprung TC. I can just see Syd, Cecil Cousins, Alec Hounslow and Henry Stone at work—using their unusual minds and hearts to conceive the TD. They knew the engine and body shape of the TC were popular and right for M.G. at that period. Without any drawings, they *thought* the TD into existence. They took a Y Type chassis with its independent front suspension plus rack and pinion steering and shortened it by five inches. They added a TC body and some hand-beaten fenders. The result was the TD. And it worked.

Sure, some diehards lamented losing those big wire wheels, but the end result was worth it. At last there was a sports car that combined roadability, classic looks and comfort.

In its three-year production run, the TD had some minor mechanical modifications that often caused some confusion. The only way to identify an M.G. properly is by the car number which is stamped in two places: on the vehicle identification plate and on the chassis itself. On T Series cars, the chassis stamping is on the front left outside chassis rail (usually called the dumb iron).

One major change came at engine number XPAG/TD/9408, when a larger clutch was specified for use on all subsequent engines. Thus the engines from that point on carry the prefix XPAG/TD2 before the actual engine serial number. It was the use of that prefix that has caused confusion about the Mark II TD.

For international class racing, M.G. had to produce a certain number of cars which all carried the same modifications as their works team. This model was called the Mark II and the modifications included an extra Andrex shock absorber at each wheel along with the standard Girling shock, twin fuel pumps, 1.5-inch carbs, the compression ratio raised to 8.1:1, and 36 mm intake valves and 34 mm exhaust valves (compared to 33 and 31 on the standard engine).

On December 1, 1952, a Mark II "appearance package" started on TC/c/22613. It included a bubble on the right-hand hood panel for the air-cleaner pipe, a "Mark II" medallion for each side of the hood and for the rear bumper, the radiator emblem was changed to black and white (a larger version of this medallion was used on the spare wheel hubcap) and the radiator slats were chromed.

The car numbers of the Mark II's carried the TD/c prefix. And that is the only acceptable proof that the car is a genuine Mark II. Most of the time the engine number had this prefix: XPAG/TD3/; unfortunately, this was not always the case.

All of these modifications resulted in a 5.5 percent horsepower increase (up to 57 hp from 54 hp). Not much of a difference, but it was noticeable. Since all of the parts were available at the time, it is not surprising that homegrown Mark II's appeared regularly.

There were fewer Mark II's produced than normal TD's, and there are those who will claim that a Mark II is worth more. It appears that many of those people who feel this way just happen to own Mark II's. Asking prices for Mark II's are generally higher, but the model really does not have enough distinction to warrant the difference.

One of the prettiest modern modifications owners do to the TD is fit wire wheels. Wire wheels, however, were never offered as an option when the

The TC caused the interest in sports cars in America. British Leyland photo.

The TC from above. British Leyland photo.

car was in production. It was only after the TF wire-wheel option was available that a TD retrofit package was made available. It depends on how much of a purist one is whether the conversion is acceptable. Original equipment or not, they sure are pretty.

In North America the Midwest dealer, S. H. Arnolt, had some TD's bodied in Italy by Bertone. More than 400 of these Arnolt M.G. coupes and convertibles were made and often appear on the market. They were heavier and slower than normal TD's but have a typical Bertone beauty to them that appeals to many. The Arnolts do not claim the same prices today as do the TD's. Perhaps it's the purist in us; whatever the reason, the Arnolt M.G. has great investment potential.

The TD was successful because it had classic looks, good performance, rode well and handled smartly; and because it continued the Safety Fast tradition in a modern manner. Anyone can drive a TD—the rack and pinion steering is easy to master, and the car is meant for enjoyable motoring.

TF

Many writers and collectors these days seem to be going out of their way to call the TF the best-looking M.G. ever made. These statements have made the TF owners happy, while making the rest of us wonder why some people waited so long to profess this wisdom. All things considered, the TF is a nice-looking car by any comparison.

The TF was an attempt to update the aging TD to keep up with heavy competition in the sports car market from the likes of Morgan, AC, Triumph, Austin-Healey and Porsche. Often called the last of the square riggers because it still bore a strong family resemblance to the prewar Midgets, the TF really was not welcomed all that warmly by the American motoring press. One journalist irreverently remarked that it looked like a TD that had been kicked in the face. The late Tom McCahill, dean of road testers, wrote, ". . . the new MG-TF is a dyspeptic Mark II imitation that falls short of being as good as the Mark II." Poor press or not, the TF has endured and has earned a special place on the M.G. family tree.

When the TD was introduced with disc wheels, the complaints from enthusiasts who loved the spidery wire wheels on previous Midgets were loud and pointed. Abingdon answered those cries by making wire wheels an option on the TF. It is possible to purchase the necessary parts to make the changeover, but be prepared to part with a thousand dollars or more—beauty isn't cheap!

The first TF's used the same basic XPAG 1250 cc engine that had done so well powering the TB, TC and TD. The public and press, however, expected more from a new model and were disappointed to discover that the Mark II TD was faster. Further, the TF was only marginally faster than a normal TD (the advantage was probably gained through the aerodynamic efficiency of the TF shape). The factory was sensitive to the complaints from the public and came up with a larger 1500 cc engine for the last 3,400 TF's. The bigger engine improved performance, and the relative rarity of the TF 1500 makes it a slightly better investment.

The 1500 cc engine received its public introduction in the record-breaking EX179 at the hands of George Eyston and Ken Miles. Together they nailed down several American and international class records for M.G. Record breaking, of course, had been a tradition at Abingdon, and Eyston was the major force behind almost every effort M.G. made over the years. The EX179 used the new XPEG block which allowed an increase in bore from the XPAG's 66.5 mm to 72 mm. Increasing the bore required a new block in order to keep the proper cylinder-wall thickness. The resultant publicity from the records was helpful in the sales of the TF 1500, and the increased performance was welcomed by everyone.

The TC was an improved TB and adapted easily to American highways. British Leyland photo.

When the TF appeared, the TC was already regarded in America with some reverence. As a result, the TF was almost an instant classic. It was purchased to enjoy and to keep. I say "keep" because the majority of buyers consciously or unconsciously realized that the TF was the last of a line. Enthusiasts knew that the next car from Abingdon would be much different. It is my theory that this sense of history resulted in a higher proportion of TF's surviving than did any other popular Midget.

On the road the TF was even more comfortable to drive than the TD. It had the same ease of handling as well as similar performance, but passenger comfort was substantially improved. Wider doors made it easier to get in and out of; once in, big, separate seats made a long journey very pleasant.

Is the TF the prettiest of all the M.G.'s? Beauty, of course, is in the eye of the beholder—or in the mind of the owner. At least the TF has the proper badge.

Serial numbers started getting really complicated with the TF. Any M.G. enthusiast worth his whits knows that the first serial number of most models prior to 1950 was 0251. He also knows that the old telephone number at the Abingdon works was 251. Now if you'll look at the beginning of this chapter you'll note that the first TF was 0501, but the break with tradition was a bit more subtle and mysterious. There was, in fact, a TF 0251; in fact, there was a TF 0250 as well. Both were prototypes and both were cut up. Why the production chaps decided to skip to 0501 is a mystery. We do know that the telephone number remained unchanged.

TF serial numbers have a complicated coding that combines letters and numbers. This system was also used on the MGA and is a great help to the careful restorer. A TF serial number such as HDP46/5694 can be decoded this way:

HD:	This is on all TF's and means that this is an M.G. two-seater, TF Series.
P:	Color: A=black, B=light gray, C=dark blue, E=mid-green, P= ivory.
4:	The first number shows the market the car was built for: 1= Home Market, RHD; 2=General Export, RHD; 3=General Export, LHD; 4=North America, LHD; 5=CKD, RHD; 6=CKD, LHD. (CKD means Completely Knocked Down and identifies a car shipped to another country for assembly.)
6:	The second number identifies the type of paint used on the car. Of six possibilities, only the three listed here are found in TF car numbers: 3=Cellulose; 5=Primed; 6=Cellulose body, synthetic wings.

As an investment, the TF rates with the TC and the TD. A wire-wheeled TF is usually worth a bit more than a disc-wheeled car, and a TF 1500 makes a slightly better investment than the 1250-engined car.

CONCLUSION

Of all the T Series cars, the TC, TD and TF are the best investments. While the TB has the same powerplant, it just does not have the replacement parts available as do the postwar cars. There is virtually nothing you can't find for a TC, TD or TF.

There are ample club activity and a great many books available for the T owner. These are cars that can be driven; with so many of them surviving, one is probably never far from a kindred (and helpful) spirit.

Early TD—note the solid wheels. British Leyland photo.

Inskip built twelve of this four-seater TD. Coming after the Y tourer, the Inskip TD gave enthusiasts the option of a sporty four-seater. Dave Jensen photo.

MODEL	YEARS PRODUCED	TOTAL BUILT	CYLINDERS	DISPLACE-MENT (cc's)	WHEEL-BASE	HORSE-POWER
TA	1936-1939	3,003	4	1292	7' 10"	52.4
TB	1939	379	4	1250	7' 10"	54.4
TC	1945-1949	10,002	4	1250	7' 10"	54.4
TD	1949-1953	29,665	4	1250	7' 10"	54.4-57
TF	1953-1955	6,000		1250		57
		3,400		1466		63

The TF from above. British Leyland photo.

Many enthusiasts regard the TF as the best-looking M.G. ever made. British Leyland photo.

CHAPTER 4
THE MGA

For those interested in joining the car hobby relatively inexpensively, the MGA offers good value for the money. With over 100,000 units built between 1955 and 1962, of which over 80,000 were originally exported to the United States, they are readily available in a wide range of condition and price. Parts are reasonably easy to obtain from several specialists and even a few still from the manufacturer (MGB commonality). The MGA shows excellent performance and handling, reasonable comfort and good potential for value appreciation.

Vividly exemplifying the maxim that "racing improves the breed," development of what ultimately became the MGA had its origin in the 24 hours of Le Mans. A factory-built aerodynamic racer provided inspiration for the MGA.

It was determined that the engine to be used in the car would be the BMC B-Series engine, thus being one of the first efforts at component rationalization across the BMC product lines. However, to optimize performance at the top end, several changes were necessary in the B-series cylinder head. These included larger valves and more "meat" around the valves. Larger carburetors and a new camshaft were also used. The B-Series engine cylinder head was designed with a heart-shaped combustion chamber (the point being between the valves). This design, unchanged in the MGA version, combined with the higher compression ratio, causes the car's tendency toward "running-on."

The MGA was built in two body styles throughout most of the production run. For the first sixteen months of production, only the two-seat roadster with side curtains and folding top was available. From late in 1956 through the remainder of production a very pretty two-seat coupe was available. This had wind-up windows, locking doors and other interior trim refinements. A total production breakdown between roadsters and coupes is not available but it is generally agreed that far fewer coupes were built, perhaps ten to fifteen percent of the total.

As with earlier series of M.G. models the MGA has a separate body and it can be removed from the chassis. The body proper and fenders are steel pressings while the doors, hood and trunk lids are skinned in aluminum alloy. Wood floorboards were still used in the MGA—old habits die hard! Exterior door handles are found only on the coupe.

The interior of the MGA is trimmed in a combination of leather and leatherette with wool carpets over jute padding. The seat cushion top and sides are leather, as is the seatback facing and edges. The rail at the top of the door and the two curved pieces aft of the door on the roadster are also trimmed in leather. The remainder of the interior trim is a matching or contrasting leatherette, commonly known as Vynide. The coupe headliner is also of a similar type of material called Lionide.

The MGA was the first production M.G. sports car to incorporate a trunk in the design. Rather small in size and containing all, or the great portion, of the spare tire (depending on the model) and the tool kit, it offers only minimal luggage space. The area behind the tilting seatbacks is, in the roadster, almost entirely occupied by the folded top structure and side curtain storage. The similar area in the coupe is more useful.

★★★ **MGA 1500**
1955-1959
Chassis Numbers HD10101-68850

★★★★ **MGA Twin Cam**
1958-1960
Chassis Numbers YDI501-2611 and YD2501

★★★ **MGA 1600 Mark I**
1959-1961
Chassis Numbers G/HN 68851-100351

★★★ **MGA 1600 Mark II**
1961-1962
Chassis Numbers G/HN2 100352-109070

The first streamlined M.G. was the very attractive MGA. British Leyland photo.

The chassis of the MGA is a very strong boxed steel design and can take much abuse. Corrosion may occur but it is normally not a major problem, except in cars from northern climates where extensive deterioration may exist under the cockpit area.

During production of the MGA, a rather extensive list of factory options was available. Whether these add very much to the value of the car is doubtful but they should be a consideration. Not all were available on all cars—literature exists showing applicability. Some of these options were: forty-eight-spoke wire wheels, various rear axle ratios, close ratio gearbox, adjustable steering column, luggage carrier, heater/defroster, tonneau cover, twin horns, radio(s), fiberglass hardtop with deluxe sliding wind screens, competition seats and front anti-sway bar.

The MGA engine block incorporated the appropriate series identification (1500, 1600, 1622) cast into the lower left-hand side. The engine number was stamped into an aluminum tag, now often missing or deteriorated, attached to the upper right-hand side of the block. The chassis number was lightly stamped into the top surface of the middle chassis cross-member, midway between the right side rail and the gearbox mount. This cross-member is subject to considerable surface corrosion resulting from a damp carpet and pad, and often the chassis number is difficult or impossible to find. The firewall data plate was stamped with the vehicle number (incorporating the chassis number) and the engine number (earlier models only).

MGA 1500

The MGA 1500 is the most common of the four basic types of MGA. Production of the roadster began in August 1955 and ended in May 1959. Actually the first MGA production chassis (number 10101, utilizing the next sequential number after the last TF-1500) was laid down on May 16, 1955. However, troubles in body production by the sub-contractor resulted in a delay in final assembly. Coupe production started very late in 1956 at chassis number 20671 and continued until May 1959. Total production of both the 1500 series coupes and roadsters totaled 58,750 units.

Chassis numbers of the MGA 1500 ranged from 10,101 to 68,850. The then standard BMC vehicle identification system incorporated prefix letters and numbers to the basic chassis number, providing information on body type, paint color and type, destination of car and so on. Details of this system (and the engine number coding) can be found in the MGA factory workshop manual or other publications and should be used to verify the correctness of the vehicle and its components. Engine numbers for the MGA 1500 were in the series 15GB and 15GD (from chassis number 61504 on).

Until 1957, the roadster top had only a single back window. Thereafter, a three "light" rear window was used, improving rear quarter visibility considerably. Taillights on the 1500 incorporated parking and brake/turn signal lamps in a single lens. Side curtains on the roadster had a hinged lower flap to permit entry to a buttoned-up car in the absence of exterior door handles. The trunk lid was opened from inside the car—no lock or exterior handle was provided. Thus, there was no lockable space on the roadster.

MGA 1600 and 1600 DeLuxe

The MGA 1600 and its extremely rare variant, the 1600 DeLuxe, were built in both roadster and coupe versions between May 1959 and April 1961. Total production of 1600 roadsters and coupes was 31,501 units. The 1600 DeLuxe commenced production in June 1960. Available records indicate that eighty-two 1600 DeLuxes were built, twelve as coupes and seventy as roadsters.

Chassis numbers of the MGA 1600 commenced with number 68851 and ended with 100351. Another new vehicle identification system was imposed on M.G. by BMC concurrent with the 1600. Again, reference to the workshop manual will assist a prospective buyer in precise identification. Engine numbers for the MGA 1600 were in the 16GA series.

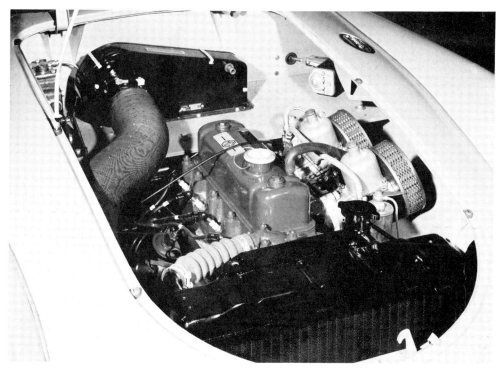

The long hood of the MGA provided good access to the 1489 cc engine, which put out 68 hp at 5500 rpm. MRP photo.

The streamlined MGA was a dramatic departure from the styling of the T series. MRP photo.

The 1600 offered a significant improvement in performance. With increases of ten percent in bhp and seventeen percent in torque, engine flexibility was noticeably improved. This engine found so much favor that a number of 1500 models have had 1600 engines retrofitted by owners. Disc brakes were fitted at the front of the 1600, thus more than compensating for the increased engine performance.

The front fender lamp was redesigned on the 1600 to provide an amber upper portion (turn signal) and a clear lower portion (parking lamp). Likewise, the rear fender lamps were reworked, resulting in a separate turn signal lamp above the previously used tail/brake/turn signal lamp. These changes were mandated by US lighting regulations. To further differentiate the 1600 from the previous model, 1600 ID badges were placed on the trunk lids and behind the engine cowl vents.

Side screens fitted to the roadster model were a much improved design in this series. The hinged flap was discarded and sliding plexiglas windows provided for entry and ventilation.

The interior of the 1600 coupe behind the seats was redesigned. The spare tire was moved entirely into the trunk. The parcel shelf was cut back to virtually nothing. The result was a rather large usable space behind the seats, suitable for a small child, large dog or three upright sacks of groceries.

The most intriguing version of the 1600 was the DeLuxe. The factory called this the four-wheel disc brake option. In truth, when production of the Twin Cam ended on June 14, 1960, approximately 400 Twin Cam chassis still remained. These were complete with the Dunlop four-wheel disc brakes, center-lock disc wheels and relocated/redesigned clutch and brake pedals and separate master cylinders. Some of these chassis were equipped with 1600 engines, gearboxes and trim and sold concurrently with the "normal" 1600 model. The "option" cost was slightly under $500.

Identification of these rare cars is readily possible by the wheels and brakes. Differentiation from a true Twin Cam in which an owner replaced the original engine with a pushrod one can be made by reference to the data plate. DeLuxe chassis numbers are listed in the 1600 (or 1600 Mark II) sequence. In addition the DeLuxe lacks the oil sump access holes in the front cross-member and access panels in the inner fenders that are found on most true Twin Cams.

MGA 1600 Mark II and 1600 Mark II DeLuxe

Production of this last model of the MGA series commenced in April 1961 and ceased in June 1962 with a final production figure of 101,081 for all models. Total production of the 1600 Mark II, again in both roadster and coupe versions, was 8,719 units. As with the 1600, a variant, the 1600 Mark II DeLuxe, was produced to use up the last of the excess Twin Cam chassis. Records indicate that 313 were built using the 1622 cc engine, of which twenty-three were coupes and 290 were roadsters. It is interesting to note that almost half of these DeLuxe versions were built in April/May of 1962—cleaning house, so to speak, for the end of MGA production.

The 100,000th MGA was a 1600 Mark II, completed on May 16, 1962. This was a left-hand-drive export roadster painted gold with gold-painted wire wheels and a special "100,000" badge attached below the normal 1600 Mark II badges.

Chassis numbers of the 1600 Mark II ranged from 100352 to 109070. Engine numbers were in the 16GC series.

The 1600 Mark II utilized an entirely different engine block than previous series. This block was used in other BMC products concurrently. Externally the only obvious difference is the "1622" cast in the block. The engine again provided a significant improvement over the previous powerplant, offering a thirteen percent increase in bhp and twelve percent in torque. However, the increase in displacement was only 34 cc.

The conveniently laid out, simple dash area of the original MGA.
MRP photo.

The MGA in a quaint English setting. Author photo.

Various body detail changes visually differentiate the 1600 Mark II from earlier models. The most striking was the front grille assembly in which the vertical bars were recessed at the bottom resulting in a more vertical appearance. Lighting regulations dictated a new taillight cluster, borrowed from the Mini. In this design, the lamps were arranged in a horizontal lens, mounted on a casting below the outboard corners of the trunk lid rather than on the fenders as previously. As had been done on 1500 and 1600 coupes and all Twin Cams, the roadster facia panel and scuttle were covered in fabric of the same type used in the rest of the interior with a chrome trim strip at the lower edge. ID badges identifying the car as a 1600 Mark II were placed in the usual places on the body.

As with the 1600 DeLuxe, the 1600 Mark II DeLuxe was an unusual version of the standard car. Using the remainder of the extra Twin Cam chassis offered a most desirable factory "option" for the aspiring club racing enthusiast. With the more powerful 1622 cc engine, the Mark II DeLuxe may be considered the ultimate MGA. The information provided earlier in the 1600 DeLuxe section applies to the Mark II DeLuxe equally, except for the engine, of course.

MGA Twin Cam

By usual standards the Twin Cam MGA was not a resounding commercial success for Abingdon. With total production of only 2,111 units (roadster and coupe) in the period September 1958 to June 1960, it did little to bolster the financial fortunes of BMC.

Chassis numbers of the MGA Twin Cam commenced with number 501 and ended with 2611. Prefix letters/numbers followed the 1956 MGA 1500 system and were in the form YD (roadster) or YM (coupe) plus 1, 2, 3 or 5. Engine numbers for the Twin Cam were in the 16GB series.

The basic chassis used in the Twin Cam was the same as used in other MGA's. Minor changes were incorporated to allow for the bulkier engine and to strengthen the chassis for the higher performance expected. The steering rack was moved forward slightly as was the radiator, spring rates were increased somewhat, sturdier axle shafts and U-Joints were used and roller bearings were fitted to the front hubs. Aside from the engine, the major chassis change was that Dunlop disc brakes were fitted all around and Dunlop center-lock disc wheels were employed. The major drawback to the system was marginal handbrake performance. Separate brake and clutch master cylinders were used, necessitating a redesigned pedal assembly.

The big change in the Twin-Cam was the double overhead cam engine. Anyone seriously contemplating the acquisition of a Twin Cam would be well advised to become very familiar with additional material available on the engine (factory workshop manual, for example).

Though based on the BMC B-series engine, the block and lower end were unique to the Twin Cam. Connecting rods and crankshaft were strengthened, the flywheel was lightened and a large-capacity aluminum oil sump was employed. It is on the upper part that the most notable changes occurred. The cross-flow aluminum alloy head with duplex chain driven twin overhead camshafts dwarfed the standard pushrod head and necessitated major relocation of components on the engine. The twin carburetors were moved to the right-hand side and an extractor exhaust system and the distributor were located on the left-hand side. An auxiliary radiator header tank was installed above the exhaust system to provide positive cooling to the head. Starter, generator and oil filter remained in their former positions.

The result of all this was an engine compartment almost completely filled with engine and components. Routine servicing became difficult due to inaccessibility. Shortly after introduction, at chassis 592, removable access panels were fitted to the inner wheel arches, making servicing somewhat simpler.

A good view of the side curtain arrangement on early MGA models. British Leyland photo.

The MGA coupe was a very handsome package. MRP photo.

The body exterior is visually identical to the MGA 1500 with the addition of the "Twin Cam" flash behind the engine bay vents and the trunk lid. In the interior, a 7500 rpm tachometer was installed and the facia/scuttle in the roadster was covered with vinyl as had been done on 1500 coupes. Competition seats, offering greater lateral body stability, were introduced as an option on the Twin Cam and were very popular.

Affectionately known today as the "Twinkie," the Twin Cam was originally conceived as a low-production sports car designed primarily for the knowledgeable competitive driver. However, as it soon found its way into the hands (and feet) of less sympathetic drivers, problems arose. With the high compression ratio used, precise attention to mixture and timing was mandatory, as was the use of at least 100 octane fuel. When these items were neglected, burned or holed pistons usually followed. In addition, oil consumption of one quart per 250 miles (for which the engine was designed) was thought to be excessive. These problems, coupled with the fact that the engine could be easily over-revved in the lower gears, soon led to a reputation for lack of reliability. The result was a decision to cease production, which occurred on June 14, 1960, when YD1/2611 rolled off the assembly line.

Interestingly enough, the solution to the piston problem was at hand, with a reduction in the compression ratio to 8.3:1. While this took a little off performance, it was not significant. At chassis number 2251, engines were thereafter fitted with the lower-compression pistons. In addition, factory rebuilt engines from then on also used these different pistons.

GENERAL CONSIDERATIONS

A very nice MGA can be purchased for the price of a basket-case TD. Steeped in M.G. history with a terrific competition background, the MGA certainly qualifies as a historic sports car. The nice thing about the MGA is that this is a car that demands to be driven and enjoyed.

For those contemplating the acquisition of a vintage sports car and unfamiliar with the road manners of such a vehicle, the MGA is an ideal car with which to explore the sheer pleasure of driving. The handling and cornering capabilities of the MGA are superb, making it perhaps the safest M.G. ever built. The well-proven rack-and-pinion steering is light, quick and responsive and if a driver is inept enough to lose it while cornering, the result is most predictable and controllable. The braking on the MGA is more than adequate, especially with the front-wheel disc brake cars (1600 and 1600 Mark II) and the all-around discs (Deluxes and Twin Cams). In essence, the MGA feels like a sports car ought to feel and performs, within its capabilities, as a sports car ought to perform. It is fast enough to satisfy most drivers today—in fact, the MGA just looks fast!

The MGA is a relatively straightforward car that can be maintained by the average owner. With its detachable body and fenders, a body-off restoration is relatively easy. The pushrod engine and drivetrain are uncomplicated, as is the braking system. With most mechanical parts (except for the Twin Cam engine bits) reasonably available, ownership of an MGA can be very enjoyable.

There are, as in the purchase of any vehicle, some considerations unique to the MGA. The wooden floor boards are most likely to be rotted out. However, this poses no real problem as they can be easily replaced. Rust, as in any ferrous metal car, is usually present and extent should be determined. Areas most susceptible are the rocker panels, the body itself around the doors and the frame under the cockpit. Due to the propensity of an M.G. to distribute oil freely in the engine compartment, corrosion is not normally a problem in the front third of the car. However, as one moves aft, one encounters it more extensively. The location of the two 6-volt batteries in series behind the seats adds to the corrosion problem. The trunk floor should also be examined for rust. If at all possible, a prospective purchaser should attempt to put the car on a lift and inspect it carefully from the underside.

The attractive MGA coupe. British Leyland photo.

Due to the bumper-mounting design, both front and rear, even the most minor encounter between a bumper and another object usually results in sheet metal damage. It is unusual to find today an MGA that has not had body repairs both front and rear in the bumper area and on the extremities of the four fenders.

Door opening angle is rather small on the MGA. This, combined with the extremely low design of the car itself, makes cockpit entry less easy than, say, the suicide-door T Series cars. The interior of the coupe can get uncomfortably warm due to inadequate ventilation. This may be a consideration only in some climates.

The design of the MGA cylinder head, though very efficient, is prone to produce cracks, generally between number two and three cylinders.

In any "investment" of this type, the ultimate monetary appreciation is rather unpredictable. Realistically, acquiring an MGA will probably not make one wealthy. The purchase of a clean Duesenberg J (also a twin cam engine!) in the mid-fifties (which one could have obtained at a comparable price to an new MGA then) would have produced a massive monetary gain. However, I do not see this happening with the MGA. Today I would prefer to consider an MGA as an investment in a car that will give pleasure of ownership with a resale value, depending on your care, that at least should return your out-of-pocket costs.

Probably the most desirable MGA, at least to the initiated, would be the Twin Cam. However, one must be prepared for extra and more expensive care than with a pushrod engine. Parts, especially engine items, are not as readily available. A Twin Cam must be regularly tuned and high-grade fuel must be used. As was mentioned previously, the lower-compression (8.3:1) pistons are highly desirable.

Clearly, the rarest MGA is the DeLuxe, especially the coupe. In the long run this should translate into a higher monetary value.

Coupes, in any of the series, in view of their lower production, generally command a price above a comparable roadster. With their unique styling somewhat akin to the Jaguar XK-120/140 coupes, they are becoming a highly desirable model of the MGA.

The MGA 1600 Mark II with its distinctive grille, different taillight and facia treatment, combined with much lower production should be more desirable than the 1500 or 1600.

Within the parameters listed above, there is little to differentiate between the 1500 and 1600. Faced with a choice of similarly equipped and conditioned roadsters, a coin flip is probably as good a decision process as any.

In summary, the MGA is an enjoyable vintage sports car, devoid of major problems, that will give many years of pleasure. Selection of a good example can be highly rewarding, at least in the satisfaction derived.

The 1600 M.G. MGA coupe with disc wheels. MRP photo.

MODEL	YEARS PRODUCED	TOTAL BUILT	CYLINDERS	DISPLACE-MENT (cc's)	WHEEL-BASE	HORSE-POWER
MGA 1500	1955-1959	58,750	4	1489	7' 10"	68-72
MGA Twin Cam	1958-1960	2,111	4	1588	7' 10"	108
MGA 1600 MK I	1959-1961	31,501	4	1588	7' 10"	80
MGA 1600 MK II	1961-1962	8,719	4	1622	7' 10"	93

The new MGA offered an honest luggage area that also housed the spare and jack. This left-hand-drive model features an optional push-button radio. MRP photo.

The lusty MGA Twin Cam. British Leyland photo.

The MGA Twin Cam engine was difficult to tune correctly and owners became disenchanted with it. Later, simple modifications made it quite reliable. British Leyland photo.

Twin cam MGA. British Leyland photo.

In 1600 Mk II guise, the MGA created 90 hp at an engine speed of 5500 rpm. MRP photo.

MGA 1600 Mk II. British Leyland photo.

Photographed below statuary symbolizing speed in London's Hyde Park, this UK-version 1600 Mk II displays the new radiator grille. Note the European headlights. MRP photo.

CHAPTER 5
THE MGB

The MGB started out on the drawing board rather than on the racetrack and was to be the first Abingdon design model with complete unit body construction, as it was felt that considerable weight savings could be achieved. Also, it was felt—incorrectly—that in the long run a complete unit body could be produced less expensively than a conventional chassis/body arrangement.

The MGB was finally introduced in September 1962, with all but two of the first 500 production cars earmarked for the American market. In a publicity letter sent to John Bond, of *Road & Track,* Tony Birt, the somewhat over-zealous advertising manager for the American importer, confidently claimed that everything except the Octagon was new. This, in fact, was a slight overstatement, as the entire drivetrain was only slightly modified from the MGA design.

The new engine was a further development of the Austin-designed B-Series unit, which traces its lineage back through a half dozen bore size increases to the 1200 cc A-40 unit of 1948. The new cylinder block incorporated siamesed cylinder bores, which meant that no water passed between the end pair of cylinders. This proved a bit of a challenge to the engineers and foundry men at the Morris Engines Branch, but in practice, posed few problems.

The crankshaft, with three main bearings of a larger diameter than those previously fitted, incorporated long-wearing copper/lead bearing throughout. The cylinder head and valve train were exactly as per the 1600 Mark II. Carburetion was still via a pair of 1½-inch SU's, but of the latest "HS" design, which were slightly less prone to losing their jet assemblies and float bowls due to engine vibrations! The original air filters were very well designed and according to Abingdon design engineers the new units added 3 bhp. This is due to the carefully designed bell-shaped air filter backing plates, which provide a certain ramflow effect inside the large, free-breathing air filter canisters. The elements were of the modern dry type. Modern owners would be well advised not to fit dress-up pancake air filters.

The MGB engine produced 95 bhp at 5400 rpm and 110 pounds feet of torque. This compared favorably with the 86 bhp produced by the last of the 1600 Mark II MGA's.

The transmission differed only in detail from the MGA unit but was fitted with a longer-wearing syncho ring on second gear which somewhat alleviated earlier complaints. It was also no longer necessary to use the MGA remote-control gear shift assembly since the driver sat farther forward in the new body. A slightly cranked gear lever fell within comfortable reach and provided for exceptionally precise shifting.

The old MGA rear suspension was fitted with wider spring perches and a lower final drive ratio, and was used successfully for some years. Although this axle assembly with its pressed steel housing and cast aluminum differential case was somewhat noisy, it was felt to be adequate for an open sports car.

The front suspension traces its lineage back to the Y type, originally designed by Alec Issigonis in 1939. In fact, the front suspension sub-frame pressings are virtually the same as the equivalent part fitted to Y, TD, TF and MGA chassis. The king pins were modified to current BMC designs and proved

★★★ MGB
1962-1980
★★★ MGB/GT V-8
1973-1976

This first version of the MGB appeared in the fall of 1962. British Leyland photo.

to be long wearing if properly greased. The old troublesome rubber A-arm bushings were retained and continued to be subject to excessive wear and deterioration. Fortunately, these are not difficult to replace. The rack-and-pinion steering was of a new design and for the first time incorporated renewable bearings. The unit was and continues to be very long wearing, but only if the rubber steering rack gaiters remain intact and properly lubricated with SAE 90 gear oil. Grease must never be injected into the system.

Spring rates were a good deal softer than on any previous Abingdon-built sports car. However, overall handling, which had always been the hallmark of M.G. sports cars, was still excellent and remained so throughout its eighteen-year production run. The only exception was 1975-76 model year cars which suffered badly due to increased ride height. Overall handling is highly predictable on the MGB thanks to slight understeering tendencies—rear end breakaway can be easily and confidently controlled.

The MGB unit body design deserves special merit for its truly rigid construction so desirable in an open sports car. Unlike many other contemporary sports cars, the MGB did not exhibit scuttle-shaking tendencies which not only could affect handling but also the overall durability of the structure. While the body is no more prone to rusting than other bodies of its type, runaway corrosion can severely weaken the body to the point where doors, particularly on the roadster model, lack sufficient clearance to close properly.

Prospective MGB buyers would be well advised to carefully inspect any car under consideration. Rust problems are first made evident by blistering paint along the door sills and lower sections of the front and rear fenders. In more advanced cases the bottoms of the doors and rear wheel arches may deteriorate as well as the tops of the front fenders where mud accumulates on top of the box section of the inner wheel arches. Roadsters left in the open with their tops down are also prone to developing rust in the main floor pan. Leaking trunk or tailgate lids can contribute to similar problems in the corners of the luggage area.

Fortunately for the current and future generations of MGB enthusiasts, badly rusted bodies can be restored to as-new condition. The key to success in this regard is in tackling the complete problem, rather than in repairing only those panels which are readily visible. The lower sills, which actually extend behind the front and rear fenders, provide a great deal of strength to the body and are made up of a number of panels forming a double box section. Some of these inner panels are even more susceptible to rust than the exposed outer panels. Most reputable MGB specialists offer aftermarket front and rear fender rust repair panels which allow the damaged outer sections to be cut away, exposing what lies underneath and avoiding the expense and effort of replacing the entire fender. The inner sill sections can then be removed and replaced as necessary with new components. The wise owner will very carefully paint and undercoat all new panels to prevent future reoccurrence.

In discussing the car as a whole, it can be safely said that the MGB, either in its roadster or GT form was in the very best Abingdon tradition. In its original guise, the B was a pure sports car built to meet the demands of that period. It is a further tribute to the men at Abingdon, that in its eighteen-year production run, the same basic car was constantly updated, both to meet the needs of the newer generation of sports car enthusiasts, and also to meet a never ending succession of American safety and clean air regulations.

Sports car road testers universally acclaimed the MGB in its earlier days for its clean lines, excellent road manners and good all-around creature comforts. *Road & Track* called it "The best engineered, best put together MG we've ever seen." As the years passed and the MGB became more and more of an institution along the lines of the Model T, VW Beetle and Morgan, journalists became perhaps rightfully more critical of the B, compared to modern

The new 1962 MGB with Old Number One in the background.
British Leyland photo.

contemporary sports and sedan cars. Performance had certainly suffered quite badly on American versions which finally produced a scant 62.5 bhp compared to 94 bhp in its pre-1968 version. Most also agree that the post-1974½ rubber safety bumpers did little to enhance the appearance of the car.

On the positive side, dozens of changes improved the durability, driveability and overall comfort of the cars while retaining most of the best handling characteristics of the earliest examples. It is perhaps unfair, yet true, to say that most changes made to meet American federal clean air and safety standards detracted from the B, while most other changes genuinely improved the breed. How then, is a prospective M.G. owner to decide which model year best meets his or her particular needs?

Perhaps the first consideration would be body type. The stylish GT version was introduced in 1965 to supplement the open tourer and was successfully produced through to the end. Unfortunately, the GT was withheld from the American market after 1974 so as to not compete with Triumph's TR7. The GT offered all-weather luxury in a tightly-knit sporting package.

The GT variant is only slightly slower through the gears due to 220 pounds of extra body weight. However, handling was slightly improved, as was top speed due to better weight distribution and aerodynamics. While the open roadsters have always been more popular than the GT, particularly in the United States, the GT's in the long run should be a better investment due to strong appeal and very limited availability.

Brief mention should be made of the most desirable of all M.G.'s—the MGBGT V-8. Introduced in 1974 for the English market only, the V-8 beautifully utilized the Rover 3.5-liter aluminum block engine. This engine was developed by Buick in the early sixties and was used in a number of mid-sized GM models of the period. Since the weight of the complete V-8 engine was less than the cast iron four, the V-8 handled beautifully and was *very* quick. Imagine the exhilaration of driving this car with 0-60 acceleration time of 7.7 seconds versus 18.3 seconds for the later federalized four-cylinder cars.

What a shame the MGBGT V-8 was never available in the American market. Triumph/Rover biased management of British Leyland decided that meeting federal pollution requirements would be cost prohibitive. Of course, the same V-8 engine was eventually smog-certified in an effort to save sagging sales for the Rover sedan and Triumph's "flying wedge." But the substantial performance boost was little help, and these models died a quiet death. One cannot help thinking that if priorities at British Leyland had been slightly different, the venerable MGB might still be in production with a V-8 engine and a fresh lease on life for the American market.

MGB's in their original 1962-67 Mark I pre-pollution and safety equipment models, will always be desirable for their purity of form. The '67 Mark I GT is a particularly desirable model, as this was the first and only year this model was available in the American market without pollution and safety equipment. Mark I cars can be identified by their simple, black wrinkled-finish steel dashboards, "eared" knock-offs for wire-wheeled cars and lack of side-marker lights, reflectors or seat headrests.

For 1963 a stronger brake lever and modified rear springs were incorporated. Overdrive, a very desirable option introduced in '63, became very popular in later years and was made standard equipment in England after June 1975, but continued to be a rare option in the US. With overdrive engaged, engine speeds were reduced by twenty percent on earlier models and eighteen percent on post-1975 models. This feature makes for most enjoyable highway cruising. While the units themselves are trouble free if kept well lubricated, the Lucas electrics and related wiring can cause annoying problems. A fiberglass hardtop was also made available this year.

The five main bearing engine, along with a standard oil cooler, was introduced in October 1964 and proved to be slightly smoother than the three

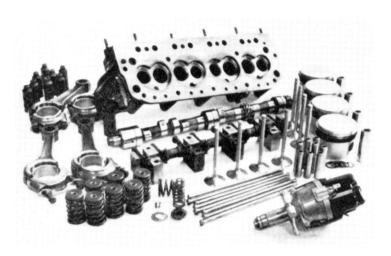

Even in its first years of production there was a full range of special MGB parts available from BMC specially developed for competition use. A "Special Tuning Manual" was also published. Bob Stone collection.

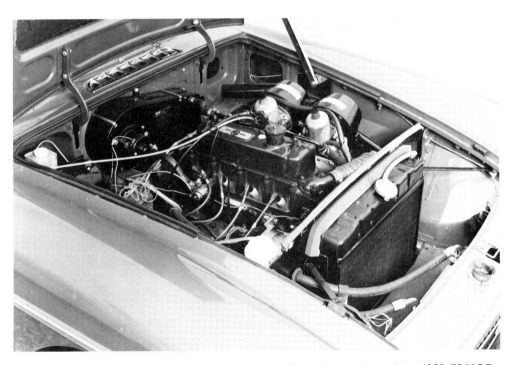

A look beneath the hood of a British version of the 1969-70 MGB. Note the oil cooler mounted in front of the radiator and the lack of pollution control pumps, hoses and so on. MRP photo.

main bearing unit it replaced. Well maintained, five main bearing engines are good for 100,000 miles between rebuilds, while the earlier units are good for approximately 70,000 miles. Well thrashed early engines are prone to crankshaft breakage. Also new for 1964 was an improved electric tach to replace the mechanical unit.

The 1966 model year marked the introduction of the stylish GT (with a twelve-gallon fuel tank). Door handles for both models were now push button. The following year a front sway bar became standard.

The only major drawback of the Series I cars is the gearbox. As mentioned earlier, the transmission was carried over from the MGA and lacks synchromesh in first gear. Also, there is quite a wide gap between second and third gear, which is not ideally suited to the rev and torque characteristics of the power unit. Second gear, however, can be used as a "starting" gear. In low-mileage or rebuilt form, the earlier gearbox is quite satisfactory, but typical high-mileage examples will have worn first and reverse gears as well as second-speed synchro rings.

Mark II cars were produced from October 1967 to October 1969 and introduced the excellent full-synchro gearbox which was to be used in only slightly altered form to the end of MGB production. Incidentally, it is not feasible to fit the full-synchro gearbox to Mark I cars as the transmission tunnel and toe board area were also modified rather extensively to accept the bulkier gearbox.

Mark II's were the last MGB's fitted with genuine leather seat facings, as well as the early chrome and vertically slatted radiator grilles. These were the first cars effected by the newly mandated American clean air and safety act, but the affects on performance at this point were minimal. Padded safety dashboards were fitted but are prone to serious cracking and lacked the refinements of later American market dash layouts. Alternators replaced the outmoded but reliable generators and the electrical system changed from positive to negative ground. (This does make it easier for current owners to fit decent modern sound systems.) Polarity can easily be reversed on Mark I cars but the later electrical tachometers will have to be reworked by a competent instrument rebuilder. Automatic transmissions were introduced as an option, but fortunately, and surprisingly, not offered to the American market. This option was withdrawn in September 1973 due to lack of demand.

The 1970 models commenced production in October 1969 and were the first M.G.'s to be influenced stylewise by the new British Leyland management. The classic radiator grille was replaced by an uninspired black recessed affair with a bright anodized aluminum surround. The center portion of the rear bumper disappeared and the license plate assembly was lowered to fill the gap. B. L. badges were prominently displayed on the front fenders and completed the indignity to the original design. Present-day owners who are not dyed-in-the-wool purists can easily retrofit early grilles and rear bumpers. A smaller leather-rimmed steering wheel also made its debut.

On the positive side, 1970 models marked the introduction of the more stylish Rostyle wheels which looked quite sharp particularly when fitted with the optional anodized aluminum trim rings. Wire wheels were, of course, still optional but in this period their popularity was waning.

Seats were now more comfortable and were easily adjustable for rake. Regrettably, the improved seats were now vinyl covered in an uninspired style. Neat rubber pads were set into the same basic bumper guards.

In 1970, British Leyland gave up the "Mark" concept of identifying successive major model variants. M.G. cars could now be identified by their model years, so designated by the sixth numeral of the chassis ID number. This system commenced with the letter "A" for the 1970 model year and continued sequentially from there. New model years generally started in October of the previous year.

The four-gauge instrument panel of early B's; and with a row of toggle switches. Bob Stone collection.

Note the similarity of grille and bumper design on the 1970 MGB and Midget. MRP photo.

As of September 1970, the folding convertible top frame was redesigned with considerable improvement by Michelotti. Earlier top frames were available either in stowaway form (which was a bit of a project to erect) or the earlier foldaway version (which was also no joy, what with its eight lift-the-dot fasteners, six press-studs, two slides, and one over center wind screen securing clip). Without a formal introduction to the mechanism, an engineering degree would be most helpful! Further improvements for '71 models were a very much improved heater system and an interior courtesy light. Telescoping hood and trunk lid stays replaced clumsy prop-rods. Nineteen seventy-two model year improvements restored the useful glovebox missing since '67 on American market cars and added face-level fresh air vents. A very neat center console with padded armrest/cubby box lid was also added. Performance for '72 was still good with only three bhp being sacrificed in the interests of clean air.

Cars for the 1973 model year were introduced with mixed blessings. The classic grille surround was back, but fitted with a tasteful black mesh grille. Also restored was a full rear bumper, and the license plate assembly was moved back to its proper position. Armrests were finally added. The seats received their last major revision, at least for the American market, and were both more attractive and comfortable. US versions also now had seat-belt buzzers installed. Roadster seats were still covered in vinyl while the last of the United States market GT's had fabric inserts. On the minus side, stiffer antipollution requirements further robbed available horsepower which was now rated at 78.5 bhp.

Nineteen seventy-four was a difficult year for the engineers at Abingdon as a flood of recently introduced or soon-to-be-introduced American regulations had to be dealt with. That model year, cars produced up through August were fitted with large black bulbous bumper guards. According to the eminent M.G. historian F. Wilson McComb, these were known within the factory as the "Sabrina" type in tribute to a well-endowed lady of the British showbiz world. If local regulations permit, these massive protrusions can be replaced with the earlier all chrome or chrome and rubber overriders. Other changes this year were the fitting of radial tires as standard and modifying the engine compartment to suit the V-8.

September 1974 marked the introduction of the most wide-sweeping change ever made to the MGB. Massive steel-reinforced polyurethane-covered bumpers were added front and rear on all models in order to meet the latest round of American regulations. In addition to minimum-impact resistance, the bumpers also had to meet standard bumper height requirements. This was accomplished by raising the entire body off its suspension by a significant 1½ inches. Not only did the bumpers increase the overall weight rather considerably, but road handling suffered badly. On a 200-foot skid pad, 1974½-76 MGB cornering capabilities were rated at 0.069 g, about on a par with typical American sedans of the period. Fortunately, the serious body roll and roll-oversteer problems were brought under control when rear antisway bars and heavier front sway bars were added for the '77 model year cars. These components can easily be retrofitted to 1974½-76 models and current owners would be encouraged to do so.

While it is possible to modify rubber-bumpered cars to chrome bumper specs (provided local regulations permit) this is a very involved project that should not be undertaken lightly. Significant structural changes were made to accommodate the rubber bumpers and some sections of the "original" fenders were cut away to provide necessary clearance. The front suspension crossmember was modified to provide increased ride height at the front which also involved changes to the steering rack and column. Rear springs were altered, as were their fixing points to the body.

As significant as the suspension changes was the further restriction on performance due to the fitting of a single carb on US models.

Interior and dash of the 1969-70 MGB. MRP photo.

This 1969-70 MGB GT was equipped with an automatic transmission. Note the map reading light above the radio speaker. MRP photo.

A short run of MGB's which still included the GT variant for the US market (except California) was produced between September and December of 1974. These were known as '74½ model year cars. These cars still incorporated twin SU carbs and produced approximately 78 bhp. The combination of a decent engine coupled with weak handling got some owners in trouble!

In January 1975 the final edition of the American smog-certified engine was introduced. This unit, producing a scant 62 bhp, was fitted with a single Zenith-Stromberg 1½-inch carb incorporating automatic choke. California versions also had a catalytic converter. The extensively revised exhaust manifold required on all American market cars is notoriously prone to cracking and is not inexpensive to replace. It is hard to believe that in the five remaining years of MGB production, Abingdon engineers were never able to correct this problem. Private owners have been known (generally against all local regulations) to circumvent the problem by fitting earlier twin carb and manifold setups. This does not restore all earlier power, as post-1975 cylinder heads for the American market also had smaller valves. English market cars continued to the end of production with twin SU's and only minimal pollution equipment. "Home" market cars were also fitted with American safety bumpers and related ride height increased from their first date of introduction. An improvement was the replacement of the two 6-volt batteries with one 12-volt unit.

Virtually all post-1975 changes were refinements that improved the car in numerous detail respects. Nineteen seventy-seven model year changes included the roll bar modifications as discussed previously. The dash for the American market received its final facelift and was really quite attractive. An electric clock was now fitted as standard equipment. The steering wheel was changed for at least the sixth time and complemented the style of the new dash.

Twin electric fans were added to American market cars while "home" market cars received only one. The thermostatically controlled fans provided fractionally more horsepower since the mechanically driven fan was no longer required. A sealed cooling system was also introduced. The overdrive switch was neatly fitted into the gear shift knob, which at last meant that all shift controls could be found in one place! Twin flush-mounted door speakers were added as standard equipment in 1978. The final American-inspired regulation came in 1980 with the fitting of an 80 mph speedometer.

Over the years a number of options not already discussed and a series of limited edition cars were produced that deserve special mention. Fiberglass hardtops for the tourers were made available by the factory throughout the production run. These were far superior to the aftermarket tops produced by a variety of specialists. The factory units were very snug fitting and can be identified by glass rear windows and aluminum-framed rear quarter windows. Chrome wire wheels were not, strictly speaking, offered by the factory. However, the American distributors were more than eager to supply them at extra cost prior to delivery. M.G.'s own Special Tuning Department made available a wide range of competition accessories, including Weber carb conversions, oversized or supplementary gas tanks, "Sebring" acrylic plastic headlamp covers (à la XKE), close-ratio gear sets, competition sway bars, heavy-duty-valved shock absorbers and a whole range of race-proven engine parts. Current owners should determine the authenticity of any odd bits prior to heaving them in the trash bin, as these factory "optional" components will one day be worth their weight in gold.

The first limited edition cars were a series of 1,000 late '67 BGT's. These "anniversary" cars were specially prepared by the American importers to commemorate the first-year anniversary of the GT variant. Special equipment was "limited" indeed, but did include a wood rim steering wheel, matching gear shift knob and photo-etched commemorative plates, which were affixed to the front fenders.

A 1971 MGB. This grille design went from 1970-72; on the '70 model the front running lights were mounted just behind the wheel well. Bob Stone collection.

British versions of the 1971-72 MGB roadster and GT. MRP photo.

The first Abingdon-inspired limited edition was the "anniversary" GT's of which 750 were built to commemorate fifty years of M.G. production. These cars were built only for the English market and were finished, appropriately enough, in British racing green with attractive gold side stripes. Handsome alloy-centered, steel-rimmed wheels were borrowed from the V-8 to complete the package.

The next limited edition offering was the LE and was available in the US. The LE was introduced in 1979 and featured any color a customer could want . . . so long as it was black! Attractive silver body stripes were added to the lower body side and special-design alloy wheels were fitted. A competition front spoiler; smaller, leather-wrapped sport steering wheel; dash plaque on the glovebox and chrome luggage rack rounded out the special equipment. This truly made for an attractive package and was the first and only time that the bumpers matched the body color. At last, they almost looked like they belonged!

The final Abingdon-built "limited edition" was truly limited as it commemorated the final 1,000 M.G.'s to be produced at Abingdon. This final edition was built, perhaps rightfully so, only for the English market. These cars incorporated all of the best features Abingdon designers could develop in eighteen years. Their only indignity was their American-inspired bumpers. Of the last 1,000 MGB's built, 420 were roadsters finished in bronze enamel and 580 were GT's finished in pewter (silver) paint. Both types were fitted with special alloy discs or wire wheels, front spoilers, special body striping and distinctive badges.

With over 513,000 cars being produced in eighteen years, a prospective M.G. owner has a great deal to choose from. No single year or variant is best suited to the tastes and needs of everyone. While this writer favors the earlier cars, there are many keen enthusiasts who swear by the later models, rubber bumpers and all.

Financial resources will ultimately be a contributing factor in one's final choice. The later cars are more expensive but also generally in better condition. If an enthusiast has reasonable mechanical aptitude and the time to devote, most repair and/or restoration work can be carried out successfully as all MGB's are relatively simple and straightforward. All MGB owners should at least be equipped with a good workshop manual and basic assortment of hand tools.

The older the model, the more carefully it should be inspected, particularly in regard to rust problems. Many cars over ten years old will exhibit some sign of rusting which may be more extensive than a cursory inspection would indicate. The older models in marginal condition are best bought as restoration projects or for planned short-term ownership. It can be a discouraging experience to keep a high-mileage clapped-out example running on a shoestring budget. On the other hand, the same example could be brought to like-new condition by a restoration enthusiast, driven for tens of thousands of additional trouble-free miles, and eventually sold, recouping all out-of-pocket expenses.

Values on early cars are largely dictated by condition but should appreciate in value over the next few years, compared to later model cars in similar condition. Late model cars, particularly in mediocre condition, should depreciate at least for a few years, but perhaps at a lesser rate than other contemporary vehicles. In the long run, all MGB's, like every other M.G. before it, will become cherished "classics" and will hopefully allow future generations the opportunity to experience the "magic of M.G."

By the 1971 introduction date of the "B," all toggle switches had been replaced with rocker switches, though the basic gauge lay-out was unchanged from the original model. MRP photo.

The highly successful 1972-model MGB raced by Group 44 out of Falls Church, Virginia. Bob Stone collection.

The GT was stylish and had the ability to carry lots of luggage or
groceries. MRP photo.

For 1973, grilles were redesigned, as seen on this MGB/GT. This was the second to last year that this fine automobile would be imported to America. Bob Stone collection.

Besides the new grille, the 1973 MGB's featured interior refinements such as armrests. Bob Stone collection.

The 1972-73 MGB (above) and MGB GT (opposite page); British
versions. MRP photos.

MODEL	YEARS PRODUCED	TOTAL BUILT	CYLINDERS	DISPLACEMENT (cc's)	WHEELBASE	HORSEPOWER
MGB	1962-1980	512,733	4	various	7' 7"	95
MGB GT V-8	1973-1976	2,591	8	3528	7' 7"	137

Two views of the 1973-74 MGB GT V-8. MRP photos.

MGB/GT V-8 with a sun roof. Ron Cover photo.

The V-8 version of the MGB/GT was a very powerful M.G. that could have been extremely popular in America. British Leyland photo.

Side view of the 1975 MGB GT. MRP photo.

The 1975 MGB roadster. MRP photo.

This special GT was available in 1975 to commemorate 50 years
of M.G. It was not sold in the USA. British Leyland photo.

Instrument area of a 1976 MGB as seen through
the nonslip, covered steering wheel. Bob Stone
collection.

Group 44 claimed its 1976 MGB Sports Car Club of America production racer developed 150 horsepower. They won a lot of races! Bob Stone collection.

A 1976 MGB. Bob Stone collection.

The much-changed 1977 B also sported a new interior design. Bob Stone collection.

The 1977 MGB was touted to have improvements in performance and fuel economy. Handling was certainly improved, though, with the addition of sway bars front and rear. Bob Stone collection.

The venerable MGB 1798 cc engine with the single SU carb. New on this 1977 model are the twin independent electric cooling fans that did not take power from the engine. Bob Stone collection.

Special on the 1977 MGB Special were stripes and the luggage rack. Bob Stone collection.

Ad copy for the 1978 MGB emphasized that the car had won the SCCA Class E national championship for six of the last seven years. Bob Stone collection.

The 1979 MGB—only one more year to go. Bob Stone collection.

The 1979 MGB. British Leyland photo.

With the 1980 model, MGB production neared half a million cars.
Bob Stone collection.

The Limited Edition MGB of 1980 featured side decals, a front spoiler, special dash plaque, luggage rack and a three-spoke padded racing-type steering wheel. British Leyland photo.

CHAPTER 6
THE MODERN MIDGET

The Midget designation was put on hold when the last TF 1500 rolled off the line in 1955. The "cheap and cheerful" tradition at Abingdon was too deeply imbedded, however, and the Midget was reborn in the middle of 1961. The car proved to be a good seller.

Badge engineering often proved to be unpopular. When those in charge decided to take the new Austin Healey Sprite Mark II and add a few octagons, calling it the new M.G. Midget, many of us were left shaking our heads. But we didn't realize just how strong the famous octagon logo really was. There were literally thousands of enthusiasts out there ready and willing to pay a premium price for the Midget over the Sprite.

The first Midget qualified as a "cute" car. Tiny, it performed well and retained a Spartan sports car image with its removable side screens and top. There is a quaintness about this early Midget that makes it more collectable.

Like the MGB, the Midget was in production for a long time and underwent many changes. Here are the major modifications that were made.

1961   Introduction in June.

1962   Late in the year the 1098 cc engine was fitted (1963 model). To cope with the increased performance, disc brakes were used at the front. Interior trim was improved and sliding side curtains were installed. The engine was notorious for its weak crankshaft. Baulk ring synchros were added to gearbox.

1964   Passenger comfort was improved with wind-up windows. More power was extracted from the engine by fitting the MG 1100 head. The dash sported a black crackle finish. By changing the rear springs from 1/4 to 1/2 elliptics, ride and handling improved. The Midget had become very civilized. This was known as the Mark II model.

1966   A mild version of the Mini-Cooper S 1275 cc engine was incorporated on the 1967 model. The passenger-compartment opening was expanded. And a much improved folding top with larger windows was introduced; other than that, this Mark III model looked about the same.

1969   The 1970 model Midget appeared late in 1969. Most of the changes were cosmetic: black rocker panels, "oval" grille, Rostyle wheels. The Mark III Midget also had an improved heater and interior lights fitted to the trunk and passenger compartment effective October of 1970.

1974   The 1975 model was now called the Mark III 1500 because of its 1493 cc engine from the Triumph Spitfire. This engine was coupled to a Morris Marina gearbox; single carb on US models. The rubber bumpers just didn't work out as well as they did on the MGB.

1979   Last Midget built in November.

Starting on 1968 models, American Midgets were fitted with emission devices that took away power. As US regulations demanded more pollution controls, performance suffered to the point that a larger engine had to be used. The Triumph Spitfire 1493 cc unit was installed in 1975 models; as you can well imagine, M.G. enthusiasts did not appreciate the change. The engine suffered from many overheating problems at first. The Midget ended its run with a less-than-satisfactory engine and ugly bumpers; I doubt that it will ever warm the heart of any collector. For 1976, revised cooling systems were incorporated.

★★ M.G. Midget 948 cc
1961-1962

★★ M.G. Midget 1098 cc
1962-1966

★★ M.G. Midget 1275 cc
1966-1974

★★ M.G. Midget 1493 cc
1974-1979

The new Midget and the last of the MGA's. British Leyland photo.

In 1971 a designer in the parent firm decided that the Midget would look better with rounded rear wheel openings. Without bothering to check with Abingdon, the styling change was made. What wasn't realized was that the rectangular opening provided strength. As a result, the rounded opening was apt to buckle at the top of the arch. Needless to say, the change back to the rectangular opening—due to '75 model US crash standards—took place without any publicity. The cars with the round opening, then, would be rarer; I don't think I'd pay any extra for one, however.

Like any car with a unibody construction, rust is a major problem. Door sills and posts are most troublesome. The floor of the passenger compartment as well as the trunk can be easily eaten away by rust. New dampers are costly and the fragile gearboxes are frequently damaged, otherwise the Midget is mechanically dependable; but always look carefully for rotten metal before buying.

In order to be comfortable, one should be under five feet ten inches tall to enjoy a Midget. These are small cars with small passenger compartments.

The Midget is a true sports car from the M.G. tradition. It will develop some sort of place among collectable M.G.'s. Like the MGB, it can be driven and upgraded at the same time. While the Midget will never be worth big money, if it's bought right, one shouldn't get hurt. It should sell for considerably less than an MGB in similar condition. It can only appreciate if bought as a used car. Since it has virtually no collector value at present, a seller should not claim collector value as a reason for a premium price. Like any used car, premium prices are reserved for cream puffs. Since the Midget invited hard use, it is difficult to imagine any cream puffs left among them.

The 1971 Midget. This new grille style first appeared in 1970. Bob Stone collection.

New colors were the highlight of the 1973 Midget—three for the outside and one new interior color. Bob Stone collection.

In Group 44 race trim, the Midget put out 125 horsepower. Bob Stone collection.

1975 Midget. British Leyland photo.

The Midget's gauge cluster was very much like its bigger brother's, the MGB. This is from a 1976 model. Bob Stone collection.

The 1976 Midget, promoted as the "lowest priced authentic sports car in America." Bob Stone collection.

MODEL	YEARS PRODUCED	TOTAL BUILT	CYLINDERS	DISPLACEMENT (cc's)	WHEELBASE	HORSEPOWER
Midget 948	1961-1962	16,080	4	948	6' 8"	46.4
Midget 1098	1962-1966	36,202	4	1098	6' 8"	55-59
Midget 1275	1966-1974	99,896	4	1275	6' 8"	65
Midget 1493	1974-1979	72,185	4	1493	6' 8"	65

From any angle there is little that has changed on the 1979 Midget, but since '76 a number of alterations had taken place. Catalytic converters were now on all US models along with different Zenith carbs and a lower axle ratio in the rear. Bob Stone collection.

Interior of a 1979 Midget. The four-spoke steering wheel was a feature of the last Midgets. Bob
Stone collection.

The last of the Midgets; 1979. British Leyland photo.

CHAPTER 7

THE MGC

The MGC looked just about the same as an MGB; the major difference was the hood and fourteen-inch wheels. In order to accommodate the larger six-cylinder engine, two distinctive bulges were added. From the front, the MGC looked very purposeful indeed.

From the beginning the MGB was a well-engineered automobile. Adding extra cylinders may well have been in the plans from the beginning. The demise of the Austin Healey 3000 hastened the introduction of the six-cylinder MGC. One should not, however, become confused here: The engine in the MGC was not the old unit from the Austin Healey 3000. It was an entirely new six-cylinder engine used in the MGC as well as a few undistinguished Leyland sedans of the period. When the MGC died, so did the sedans—and that engine.

If you doubt the power of the press, then consider what it did to the MGC. Most of the motoring journals did dreadful reports on the car, and the MGC just never recovered from them. Road testers were particularly upset with the handling: The added weight (340 pounds more than the MGB), mostly in front, created considerable understeer (the front end tends to continue in a straight line when turned). The other major criticism was that while the top speed of the car was most impressive, low-speed performance did not match the four-cylinder MGB. Both of these problems probably could have been solved by Abingdon's development staff, but it wasn't given the chance.

The factory did change the rear end gearing on later cars which corrected the low-speed performance deficiency. It never was able to cope fully with the understeer. No doubt having all suspension components in top shape helps. One could also try different types of tires and pressures as well as competition shock absorbers.

Other features of the MGC were modern telescopic shocks, front torsion bars (instead of coil springs), larger front discs and smaller but wider drums in the rear.

If an MGC can be purchased for the same price as an MGB in similar condition, then it should be a good buy with good investment potential. Unfortunately, there are those who are convinced that it is extremely rare and valuable. Last year I spotted an unregistered MGC/GT in Maine and stopped to check it out. It was all there but rusted out as only Maine cars can rust. It ran quite well as M.G.'s are apt to do. It was, indeed, restorable, and I was most interested until the owner informed me that it was a rare racing M.G. and very valuable. Well, we didn't get together because my top offer would have been one-third of his asking price, and I refused to insult him. The car is still there getting rustier by the week.

When you consider that the MGC could do a genuine 120 mph in top gear, you know that this was a real performer on the highway. The V-8 topped it by 4 mph, but the MGC had nothing to be ashamed of in the top speed department: It could go! The fastest four-cylinder MGB only reached 105 mph.

Parts can be a problem on the MGC, especially the front suspension and brakes, but don't hesitate to buy an MGC if priced right. Like the MGB, it can be enjoyed for years as its classic status grows. The MGC is a performance automobile destined to be admired.

★★★ MGC
1967-1969

The six-cylinder MGC was a victim of bad press and was never developed to its fullest potential. British Leyland photo.

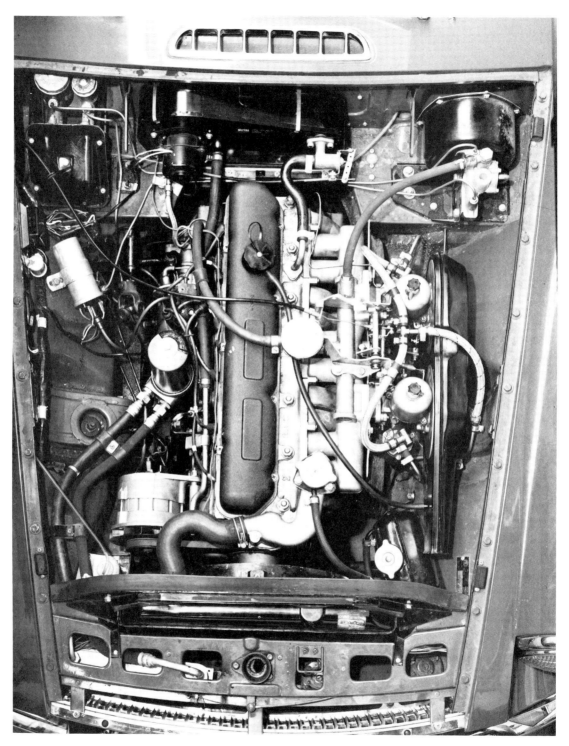

Squeezing a six-cylinder engine into the space of the MGB's four
made for a very tight fit. MRP photo.

The two pronounced hood bulges of the MGC are clearly evident here. MRP photo.

MODEL	YEARS PRODUCED	TOTAL BUILT	CYLINDERS	DISPLACE-MENT (cc's)	WHEEL-BASE	HORSE-POWER
MGC	1967-1969	8,999	6	2912	7' 7"	145

MGC in racing dress. British Leyland photo.

The "C" saw some competition usage, here in endurance racing trim at a British venue. MRP photo.

"For Space . . . For Grace . . . For Pace" is what the ads for the stylish M.G. family cars from the late-thirties said. And they were truthful at a time when there were no governmental regulations requiring it. These handsome cars were the largest and most luxurious that M.G. had ever made.

First was the SA with a wheelbase of more than ten feet. This successful model was offered in a choice of four-door saloon, four-seat Tickford drophead coupe and as a four-seat Charlesworth tourer. The saloon was the most common with the tourer being the rarest. The Tickford would take the beauty prize, but any version of the SA was very nice-looking.

With a big two-liter engine producing 78.5 bhp, the performance was very acceptable. M.G. was always a pioneer in four-up sports motoring in comfort, and the SA certainly continued that tradition.

To the untrained eye, the VA doesn't look much different from the SA. Back in 1937, that was the idea. By putting a four-cylinder engine in a slightly smaller car, M.G. was able to offer space, grace and pace to the public for less money. A VA isn't an SA, but it filled the need at the time.

The octagon was Cecil Kimber's obsession; some say his blood veins were so shaped. Whatever the reason, he loved them. He tried octagonal headlamps and even a steering wheel. The most-octagon-possessing M.G. was the VA. An accurate count is probably impossible, but it does hold the record.

The VA was offered in the same body styles as the SA. As you might suspect, the Tickford version of the VA was the prettiest. The tourer wouldn't even enter the beauty contest as it just didn't work out as an effective design.

The smaller engine in the VA meant that it came up short in the performance department. The general good looks combined with the superior roadability of the car, however, made it a winner. It still is.

The average car enthusiast always equates M.G. with "small" or even "tiny." Even today, people are awestruck at the sight of the WA and find it difficult to believe that a car this big could be an M.G.

The WA was more than a bored-out SA. Slightly larger, heavier, more powerful, the WA was further distinguished by even more luxury than was present in the others. The WA came along at the right time in that it was a motoring concept that had matured. Unfortunately, it also came along at the wrong time as World War II put a stop to the project. Too bad, for this 2.6-liter-engined car was beauty and bigness rolled into one.

When considering the SA, the VA or the WA, one must keep the terms "luxury," "comfort" and "safety" uppermost in the mind. These handsome saloons were not designed as out-and-out sports cars, but rather for space, grace and pace—which they provided very well.

M.G. club jargon groups these cars together as S, V, W. From a collector's viewpoint, there isn't much to distinguish them. Rarer body styles are probably worth more. Since fewer WA's were made, they will bring a higher price than either an SA or a VA. SA's, too, seem to be priced just a bit more than VA's. Condition, of course, is the prime influence, and the prices on these three saloons really are not all that far apart from one another. As a price guide, these cars seem to sell somewhere between TC's and TD's.

★★★★ SA
1936-1939
★★★★ VA
1937-1939
★★★★ WA
1938-1939

SA Tickford Drophead Coupe. British Leyland photo.

However, in strictly economic terms, the restoration of one of these, especially the S and the W, is hard to justify. The costs, particularly if much professional work is required, are comparable to what one would pay to do a Bentley/Rolls-Royce/Jaguar of that vintage. The value of the completed car is just not there simply because it is an M.G., not a Bentley/Rolls-Royce/Jaguar. It is perhaps unfortunate but it is true and buyers should be aware of this anomaly in the "cheap and cheerful" M.G. thinking.

SA saloon. Author photo.

MODEL	YEARS PRODUCED	TOTAL BUILT	CYLINDERS	DISPLACE- MENT (cc's)	WHEEL- BASE	HORSE- POWER
				2288		
SA	1936-1939	2,738	6	2322	10' 3"	75.3
VA	1937-1939	2,407	4	1548	9'	54
WA	1938-1939	369	6	2561	10' 3"	95.5

VA saloon. Author photo.

The WA was the largest M.G. ever made. Ron Cover photo.

M.G. sedans are nothing new. In the prewar days the M.G. Car Company produced some gorgeous sedans in the SA, VA, WA range for the sporting motorist who required an enclosed car with four seats.

Interestingly enough, the Y Type was really a prewar design: It probably would have been in production by 1940 if the war had not come along when it did. Introduced in 1947, the YA sedan was an innovative M.G. because it featured two improvements previously unknown among M.G.'s at that time: independent front suspension along with rack and pinion steering.

The engine used was the familiar XPAG unit currently in service on the TC Midget, except a single carburetor was installed. One carb plus coachwork that added 500 pounds meant that performance was down. Nevertheless, this pretty little sedan sounded and handled as an M.G. should, and it proved to be a popular motorcar—especially in England.

The Y Type was a sedan produced by a factory that was concerned with its image. Although not high-priced, it had many luxuries usually found on only very high-priced cars: leather interior, walnut trim, sunroof, plenty of ashtrays and a rear window curtain. It was a class automobile for a reasonable price.

Today many owners of classic two-seater M.G.'s are restoring Y Types as complements to their roadsters. While a total of 7,459 YA and YB sedans were built, many were lost to salvage companies which used them either for scrap or for T Type parts. It is extremely difficult to guess just how many survive. Those that are left seem to be in the same price range as MGA's. Except for YA rear axle components, parts are available, and Y Types are enjoyable motorcars.

There really was not much difference between a YA and a YB. The YB utilized a more modern hypoid rear axle as fitted to the TD along with the TD's fifteen-inch wheels, heavier shocks and a sway bar; these improvements gave the Y Type better handling and an improved ride. Both the YA and YB looked the same and had the same virtues; it just doesn't make sense that one would be more valuable than another. Y Type sedans are still affordable and make a great addition to a classic M.G. stable.

An even better Y Type for investment purposes would be the Y tourer. Only 877 of these two-door, four-passenger tourers were made. Since they were not very popular during their production period, not very many seem to have survived. The works installed the standard TC engine in the Y tourer, but the twin carbs didn't give it much of a performance edge; yet, the car did give four people the opportunity to enjoy top-down motoring in comfort. Priced at more than an MGA but less than a TD, the Y tourer is a good investment. Its rarity (and usefulness), rather than improved looks, makes the YT worth more than either the YA or the YB.

The ZA Magnette was introduced at the 1953 motor show and was a case of blatant badge engineering; that is, the parent company (now British Motor Corporation) took an existing model (the Wolseley 4/44), put an M.G. grille on it and introduced it to replace the more sedate Y Type.

Sticking the badge on a Wolseley was not particularly popular with M.G. enthusiasts, but the car soon caught on largely because of its new 1489 cc

★★ YA
1947-1953

★★ YB
1947-1953

★★★★ YT
1947-1953

★★ ZA Magnette
1953-1956

★★ ZB Magnette
1956-1958

★★ Magnette Mark III
1959-1961

★★ Magnette Mark IV
1961-1968

★★ MG 1100
1962-1967

★★ MG 1300
1967-1971

★★ M.G. Metro
1982-

Y Tourer. Author photo.

engine that was destined for later use in the MGA. The ZA continued the M.G. sedan tradition of luxurious appointments (walnut and leather were freely used) in an affordable sporting sedan.

Larger carbs on the ZB gave that later car an extra 8.4 horsepower, which combined with a more favorable rear end ratio to give this car improved performance along with wider acceptance. The last improvement in the ZB was the Varitone version which featured two-tone colors and a larger rear window.

Although the ZA and ZB have their differences, these changes are not notable in the collector car market. Really good examples of either will sell for less than an MGA. Pristine cars will hold their value, but unless the car comes to you that way, it could be an expensive restoration. I think most enthusiasts would be happier with an MGA unless they're looking for a family car addition to an M.G. collection.

The ZA and ZB were great rust developers. While these sedans may not be the all-time M.G. rust champs, they certainly must rate in the top three.

One would have to be out of his octagon-head to buy either a Mark III or a Mark IV Magnette as an investment. This was badge engineering at its worst—and neither was built in Abingdon. I suppose that if a mint car with extremely low mileage turned up at a bargain price, it might be worth buying—but only because it was an old car in unusual original condition.

Now the front-wheel-drive MG 1100's and MG 1300's are a bit different. Both M.G. versions of the Morris 1100 econobox provided a semblance of sporting motoring. The Hydrolastic suspension provided remarkable handling; but poor reliability caused this model's demise. Perhaps its most redeeming quality is a proper (almost!) M.G. grille. This really is a pretty-good-looking car that may prove popular with future collectors. The major difference between the two models was in the engine size.

These boxy little cars were raced in England and won a couple of major races. They are very prone to rust. If you can find a whole car, I doubt that it would be very expensive. I'd be willing to bet that it might appreciate as well.

The current M.G. Metro is another case of badge engineering on the new Mini Metro from Leyland. It couldn't be produced in Abingdon because the works had been torn down. The car has received highest marks from the European motor press. The car must be considered here because, as the first of a new breed of M.G., it is bound to be of interest to future collectors. Abingdon is gone, but the M.G. is very much alive in this new sedan.

Two views of the Y saloon. British Leyland photos.

A ZB saloon with the Abingdon skyline in the background. Author photo.

ZA saloon. British Leyland photo.

Z Magnette. British Leyland photo.

Magnette Mk IV. British Leyland photo.

The large panel on the dash of early Sports Sedans was an almost cardboard-like material. Bob Stone collection.

MODEL	YEARS PRODUCED	TOTAL BUILT	CYLINDERS	DISPLACE- MENT (cc's)	WHEEL- BASE	HORSE- POWER
YA	1947-1953	6,158	4			
YB	1947-1953	1,301	4			
YT	1947-1953	877	4			
ZA	1953-1956	12,754	4			
ZB	1956-1958	23,846	4			
Magnette Mark III	1959-1961	15,676	4			
Magnette Mark IV	1961-1968	13,738	4			
MG 1100	1962-1967	116,827	4			
MG 1300	1967-1971	26,240	4			
Metro	1982-	---	4	1275	7' 4 2/3"	----

A front view of the 1966 MG Sports Sedan. Bob Stone collection.

Later models of the 1100 changed to a more-presentable panel for the dash. Bob Stone collection.

The MG1100 was a sporty version of the Morris 1100. British Leyland photo.

CHAPTER 10
BEFORE THE M TYPE

Well, we're starting to get somewhat esoteric at this stage of the book. We've now reached the point where your chances of obtaining a car discussed in the next two chapters are about as good as my chances of winning the Indy 500 next year.

But you need to know about these cars. Our collector mentality makes us think that there is an undiscovered example out there and that we'll find it someday. Good hunting!

There are those who would like to go back to William Morris' bicycle days to search for an M.G. connection—perhaps octagonal axles or serial numbers beginning with 0251—but one does have to draw the line somewhere. Besides, this isn't a history book so I'll leave that to writers of history.

The first M.G.'s carried the Morris Bullnose radiator instead of the distinctive radiator more readily identified with the marque. The 14/28 Super Sports was the first car that was put into any sort of production. It had a four-cylinder engine and was available in either open or closed body style. These cars were all built in Oxford (Cowley) since the move to Abingdon didn't take place until 1929. Like many later M.G.'s, the 14/28 relied heavily upon Morris parts.

The use of Morris parts, plus special bodies, plus M.G. pride of workmanship that became a major part of the M.G. tradition added up to a car that was quickly accepted. In 1926, the radiator became more recognizable as belonging to an M.G., and over the next couple of years evolved into that now classic shape. The familiar octagonal badge first graced the front of an M.G. in 1927; it, too, evolved quickly into the badge we all know.

The 14/28 sort of "became" the 14/40. If having octagons makes an M.G., then the 14/40 certainly qualifies—It has plenty of them. Although these cars are rare, I have known of two to change hands in America recently. You just never know what will turn up in the old car hobby.

The 18/80 was pure M.G. It was more M.G. design than anything else. Add to that the fact that many of them were built in Abingdon and that the 18/80 really looked like an M.G., and you have an important car. All of these pre-Abingdon cars are of extreme historical significance.

The 18/80 was the first of the M.G. six-cylinder cars, and appeared at the 1928 motor show. Like most early manufacturers, M.G. offered a wide variety of body styles. On top of that, several bare chassis were sold so that a customer could have a special body built; this practice was not at all uncommon in the pre-World War II days.

The 18/80's proved very popular even though M.G. did not flood the market with them. People who could afford cars bought them; unfortunately, not many people could afford them. Happily, Kimber got the idea: Give them a car they can afford. Thus the M Type was born.

★★★★ 14/28 Super Sports
1924-1926

★★★★ 14/28 Flat Radiator and 14/40
1926-1929

★★★★ 18/80
1928-1933

1924 M.G. British Leyland photo.

A flat radiator 14/28 four-seater from 1927. British Leyland photo.

1928 14/40 Tourer. Author photo.

MODEL	YEARS PRODUCED	TOTAL BUILT	CYLINDERS	DISPLACEMENT (cc's)	WHEELBASE	HORSEPOWER
14/28 Super Sports	1924-1926	About 400	4	1802	8' 6" and 9' 0"	---
14/28 and 14/40	1926-1929	About 900	4	1802	8' 10 1/2"	35
18/80	1928-1933	736	6	2468	9' 6"	60

1927 four-seater 14/40. British Leyland photo.

14/40 saloon. British Leyland photo.

1930 18/80 six-cylinder M.G. British Leyland photo.

18/80 Mark II two-seater with dickey seat. Wiard Krook photo.

CHAPTER 11
THE RARE RACERS

Back in 1927 was the first record of an M.G. sports car winning a race. It wasn't a very important race, but it was the beginning of a competition record unmatched in the annals of sports cars.

The first major competition effort by M.G. was at Brooklands, England's most prestigious track. Gold medals were awarded to five M Type Midgets for their performance in the JCC High-Speed Trial in June of 1929. For the next five years, competition was a by-word (which made M.G. a buy-word) at Abingdon. Again at Brooklands in 1930, M Types won the team prize in the grueling Double Twelve race which saw the cars on the track for twenty-four straight hours.

These Double Twelve wins caused the factory to produce some 12/12 M Types which were duplicates of the cars in the 1930 race. These were all fabric-bodied cars with traditional M.G. colors: chocolate brown bodies and cream fenders. It isn't known exactly how many 12/12 M Type Replicas were built by the factory. Since duplicates wouldn't be all that difficult to make today, I am avoiding listing this version separately. A genuine 12/12 would be very desirable, but one must check very carefully before buying or risk winding up with a replica Replica.

At that same Brooklands race in 1930 was the highly touted but monumentally unsuccessful 18/100 Six Mark III Tigress. It was big and hairy-looking with cycle wings all around and all sorts of racing accouterments. None of these helped, however, and the Tigress became M.G.'s racing car failure. I doubt that anyone noticed (except the company's accountants), because the Midgets had done so very well.

In the twenties, big supercharged Bentleys were having their way at the TT, Le Mans and Brooklands. Cecil Kimber knew he had a successful road car in the 18/80 and was convinced that it could be modified to compete with the Bentleys. H. N. Charles was the chief engineer on this project as he was on all of the subsequent M.G. racing cars through 1935.

Charles used much of the existing 18/80. Major changes included a close-ratio transmission coupled to a highly modified engine. The engine utilized dry-sump lubrication and twelve spark plugs (two per cylinder). As with all pre-1936 M.G.'s, brakes were cable operated, but on the 18/100 the driver could adjust them from the cockpit. There were two electrical systems and two fuel systems to serve as back-up.

The Tigress was a good car that could, perhaps, have been developed. The enthusiasm (both at the factory and with the motoring public) swung to the M Type Midget, and the project was dropped.

Five of these Tigresses (also sometimes known as Tigers) were built and three are definitely accounted for. Maybe the other two have survived; if so, let's hope they're found and brought back to an original state.

In 1930, a successful racing driver by the name of George Eyston wanted to try to capture the world's hour record for 750 cc cars. Two friends of his, Ernest Eldridge and Jimmy Palmes, had successfully modified an M Type engine to produce some amazing amounts of power. Imagine their delight when they visited Abingdon and found that the experimental shop there had a chassis ready and waiting.

★★★★★ 18/100 Six Mark III Tigress
1930

★★★★★ C Type Midget
1931-1932

★★★★★ J3 Midget
1932-1933

★★★★★ J4 Midget
1932-1934

★★★★★ K3 Magnette
1932-1934

★★★★★ NE Magnette
1934

★★★★★ Q Type Midget
1934

★★★★★ R Type Midget
1935

18/80 Tigress racing model. Birtwhistle photo.

Designated EX120, the car Eyston drove eventually took the record at Montlhery in France at speeds up to 103.13 mph. This impressive accomplishment firmly established M.G. in the competition world.

Based on the record car, the C Type was a successful race car. Two months after the germ of the idea, fourteen C Types were ready for the 1931 Double Twelve. They promptly won and won big.

C Types were the first of the Midgets to have the double-humped curve for wind deflection. Some C Types were supercharged, but it was possible to have normal carburetion as well. The distinctive Edsel-like nose had its roots with the EX120 record breaker. The record attempts were in the bitter cold of February in 1931, and the crew was having problems with carbureter icing caused by the combination of alcohol fuel and the low temperatures. Cecil Cousins and Gordon Phillips fabricated a nose section out of an oil drum. This new nose became an air preheater and saved the day. The C Type was offered with an EX120 nose nicely done in the bodyshop; when removed, the traditional square radiator was firmly and beautifully in place.

The C Type amassed a very impressive competition record and established M.G. as the car to beat. There were forty-four C Types made and thirty-five are known at this writing.

The J3 and J4 are, of course, based on the J1 and J2 chassis. The J1 and J2 were normal passenger cars; if the factory could win races with a version of these cars, then sales were bound to go up. That thinking holds true today regardless of the remoteness of the relationship between the road car and the race car. Back in the thirties, however, that relationship was much closer than it is today. Before leaving the chassis, one should be reminded that the C Type chassis design, which was based on EX120, served every Midget through 1949.

While not a pure racing car, the J3 is included here because it had a short production run; it was supercharged; and it won its share of honors in rallies and trials. Further, a J3 was used at Montlhery in December of 1932 to capture all of the 750 cc speed records for twelve to twenty-four hours. That was a major feat, especially when one considers that the J3 wasn't much more than a J2 with a big Powerplus supercharger stuck on the front. And it did it without the benefit of a special crankshaft.

Only twenty-two J3's came off the line at Abingdon, and the whereabouts of seventeen are known.

The J4 was a real racing car. Uncommonly fast for the size of its 746 cc engine, it proved to be a handful to drive. Since the engine was supercharged and free revving, something had to be done about the fragile crankshaft. Fully counterbalanced, solid billet crankshafts were used. The result was a bomb loaded with power that only a select group of drivers could handle. Unfortunately, there weren't as many drivers as there were cars. But the history of all nine cars that were built is well-documented.

Known as the "Magnificent Magnette," the K3 probably is the most desirable M.G. ever built. Born and bred in and for competition, the K3 was an instant success. Its first major appearance was in the 1933 Mille Miglia. Not only did the George Eyston/Johnny Lurani K3 win its class outright, but the team from Abingdon also won its class. Win followed win, and the K3 served to make M.G. world famous.

The 1933 K3 came in the more familiar slab tank body while the 1934 model featured a pointed tail; both versions were extremely handsome. Since the cars were designed for road racing, the bodies were Spartan two-seaters. When the K3 went out of production, many owners made yearly modifications to make their cars competitive: They often fitted new single-seat bodywork for more speed.

Power for the K3 came from a 1097 cc engine with a supercharger. The transmission was the effective preselector. Road equipment such as fenders

M Type Midget Double Twelve. Author photo.

and lights were fitted. Like most M.G.'s of the period, a customer could buy a car without a body—at least two of the thirty-three were sold this way.

It must be the K3's great competition history that makes it so popular among collectors. It truly is *the* M.G. to own and to know about. With thirty-three K3's having been built in 1933 and 1934, the K3 is not the rarest M.G., but it is the most desirable. Of those original thirty-three cars, there are at least six unaccounted for at this time.

The K3 clearly dominated British sports car racing in 1933; one, in the hands of the famous Tazio Nuvolari, won the prestigious Tourist Trophy close to the end of the racing season. As is so often the case when one car dominates, rule changes are made to give other marques a chance. In 1934 then, the TT rules forbade superchargers. Never ones to give up easily, the racing and development shop responded to the rules change with the NE Magnette. The major change was in the engine which was enlarged to 1271 cc. The car was, of course, based on the NA chassis but with a racing body complete with pointed tail.

Despite a tight deadline, the NE's were ready for the 1934 TT, and Charlie Dodson won it. There were just seven NE's built which makes it the rarest racing M.G. All seven are accounted for.

Close behind the NE for rarity is the Q Type Midget. Only eight of these were made: The whereabouts of all eight has been established. The Q Type utilized chassis and engine bits from the N, P and K which were all produced concurrently at Abingdon.

Using the four-cylinder engine from the P combined with a new Zoller supercharger, the wizards of Marcham Road (that's where gate 3 was located in Abingdon) extracted an easy 100 hp from the 746 cc engine. And, when tweaked fully, the factory dyno went over 140 bhp. If the Q Type had never done a thing on the track (it did—class wins and several speed records), then certainly its engine alone would deserve museum space.

M.G. racing cars reached their heights with the 1935 R Type Midget. This was a true *monoposto* racing car which *might* have been developed into a genuine Grand Prix car.

The R Type featured a wishbone frame and torsion bar suspension which was fully independent. The engine was the bomb for the Q Type.

The R may have been the most advanced race car of its time. Unfortunately, it was never able to develop properly. The economists among you readers will quickly realize that the height of M.G.'s racing program was taking place during the Great Depression. Racing was not making money for the company, so it was dropped: not curtailed; it was cut. With the cut went any further development of the famed R Type. Ten were made and there are none missing at this time; chances of owning one are very remote.

In addition to these factory cars, there were many racing specials made over the years. Basing their modifications on road cars, owners fit special bodywork and raced the cars all over the world. Racing specials are very important cars to collectors; especially to those who want to participate in vintage sports car racing. The value of any racing car is enhanced if (and only if) the history of the car can be clearly documented.

After World War II, the factory was involved (sometimes directly, sometimes indirectly) in racing. There were some favored drivers who received factory support. The cars involved included TD's, MGA's, Y Types, Z's, MGB's, Midgets and MGC's. They raced all over the world from Le Mans to Sebring. There can, of course, only be a limited number of "factory" cars. Again, insist upon full documentation when offered a car with this sort of history.

M.G. did not become the international synonym for sports car because it was a cute two-seater. No, its reputation was earned in wheel-to-wheel racing. For my money, any car with a genuine racing history is worth more than a road car, and the most desirable of all are these rare racers from Abingdon.

C Type Midget. British Leyland photo.

C Type from the rear. Author photo.

MODEL	YEARS PRODUCED	TOTAL BUILT	CYLINDERS	DISPLACEMENT (cc's)	WHEELBASE	HORSEPOWER
18/100	1930	5	6	2468	9' 6"	As tuned
C	1931-1932	44	4	746	6' 9"	As tuned
J3	1932-1933	22	4	746	7' 2"	As tuned
J4	1932-1933	9	4	746	7' 2"	As tuned
K3	1932-1934	33	6	1087	7' 10 3/16"	As tuned
NE	1934	7	6	1271	8'	74
Q	1934	8	4	746	7' 10 3/16"	As tuned
R	1935	10	4	746	7' 6 1/2"	As tuned

The J3 was supercharged. British Leyland photo.

The supercharged, doorless, J4 racing car, British Leyland and
Tiche photos.

K3 Magnette racing car. British Leyland photo.

The 1934 boat-tail K3. Herlin photo.

The author at the wheel of the 1934 Tourist Trophy winning NE.
The present body differs from that fitted in 1934. Pat Green photo.

The winning NE at the 1934 TT. British Leyland photo.

While many special builders made single-seaters out of production M.G.'s, the R Type was the only M.G. conceived as a true *monoposto*. British Leyland photo.

CHAPTER 12
FAKES, FORGERIES AND REPLICAS

When is a car not a car? As time goes on and memory dims, there are bound to be truths stretched. The old car hobby is not immune to the sort of forgery that goes on in many other collector fields such as art and antiques.

The most expensive M.G.'s are the rare racing models. Since most of them were based upon production car components and built upon production car chassis, fakes and forgeries are not at all difficult to construct. A C Type on a D Type chassis or a Q Type on a P Type chassis or a K3 on a K chassis would be an easy chore considering the sort of talent that abounds in the hobby today.

I have seen some of these fakes and admire the craftsmanship. I can accept them for what they are. Further, I have no quarrel with anyone who does this as long as there is no intent to misrepresent the fake as the real thing. My guess would be that ninety-nine percent of the people constructing these forgeries have no intention of fooling anyone. The problem comes when one of these fakes changes hands.

Let's say someone buys an excellent fake K3 to drive and enjoy. He owns it for ten years, then dies one day. To settle his estate, the fake K3 is put into an antique car auction. Giving everyone the benefit of the doubt, the fake K3 is sold in the auction for what it is: a fake. But like so many cars sold at auction, it stays on the auction circuit, changing hands at every one of them for more and more money. You can bet that somewhere along the way it will change description from being an excellent fake to the real thing.

That is the danger of fakes and forgeries, and that is why the smart buyer demands full documentation. Insist upon papers and photos. Demand to be shown chassis numbers in proper places. Do not accept partial numbers and restamps. Further, search out recognized M.G. historians and collectors; most of these people do know where the genuine rare race cars are located. Be especially wary of recently discovered cars. It's a tough world in the old car hobby, and enthusiasm can easily blind the most careful buyer.

When is a car not a car? I know that many readers winced when I used the terms fake and forgery. Well, there doesn't seem to be a more descriptive word for taking, say, a P Type chassis and making a Q Type out of it. Some would have me say "replica," but I can't. A replica is created out of mostly new parts and is meant to look the same as the real thing. I maintain that the intention is to fool someone with the fakes. True, one may not be doing it for profit. There are quasi-honorable reasons for building a fake: keeping the marque on the track, historical research, pride of craftsmanship. The bottom line, however, is that the builder is trying to fool someone.

There are those who claim that if you have a major part or two of a genuine car, you can build a new car using those parts and then claim you have the car. I don't subscribe to that concept either. How major must the parts be? How many major parts must one have? Would a chassis be enough? I ask you, does a skeleton make a man?

When buying a car, it is very legitimate to ask how much of it is original. With a worldwide emphasis upon concours winners, there has been a trend to replacing old parts with new. Worn parts must be replaced; that is a natural and safe thing to do. But to discard a serviceable, say, fender because it is dented

TF Replica. Author photo.

is much the same as amputating a man's arm because it's broken. That fender is a part of the car's history, and I think it should be preserved if at all possible. When one buys a historic car, one buys history. Want a *new* car? Go to your corner dealer.

On the market today are several fiberglass kit cars that resemble the TD Midget. These body and interior kits are designed to fit on the older Volkswagen Beetle floor pan without very much trouble. The end result is an eye-catching car that is no more a sports car than my typewriter table. Handling winds up being worse than it was on the old Beetle, and you know what Ralph Nader had to say about that.

PARTS AND SERVICE SOURCES

AUCTION RESULTS, VALUE GUIDES
Gold Book
910 Tony Lama St.
El Paso, TX 79915

Kruse Classic Auction Co.
Kruse Building
Auburn, IN 46706
219-925-4004

Water Gard Publishing Co.
P.O. Box G.G.
Gainesville, GA 30601
404-534-1811

AUTO MATS
Auto Mat Co., Inc.
225A Park Ave.
Hicksville, NY 18801

BABBITING
Wola Sharp
98 Fieldpoint Rd.
Newark, OH 43055
614-522-2303

BRAKE CYLINDER REBUILDING
White Post Auto Restorations
 Co., Inc.
White Post, VA 22663
703-837-1140

CARBURETOR & FUEL PUMP REBUILDING
Britain West Automotive
 Specialties, Ltd.
Pleasant Ridge Rd.
R.R. 2
Brantford, Ont. N3T SL5
Canada

James E. Taylor
1222 Harned Dr.
Bartlesville, OK 74003

CAR COVERS
Beverly Hills Motor Parts
200 S. Robertson Blvd.
Beverly Hills, CA 90211

M.G. Mitten
44 S. Chester
Pasadena, CA 91106
213-681-4531

Reliable Car Accessories
1751 Spruce St.
P.O. Box 5710 C-CO6/79
Riverside, CA 92507

Warren Cox
P.O. Box 216 CC
Lakewood, CA 90713

CHROME AND METAL PLATING
Classic Chrome
2430 Washington St.
Boston, MA 02119
617-445-3475

Mike Drago
141 E. St. Joseph
Easton, PA 18042
215-252-5701

Qual Krom
28 Orchard Place
Poughkeepsie, NY 12601
914-229-7792

Swirin Plating Service
535 Indian Rd.
Wayne, NJ 07470

ENGINE REBUILDING
Bill Drake's Engine Shop
259 Lee Rd.
Rochester, NY 14606
716-458-0217

EXHAUST SYSTEMS
Burton Waldron
Box C
Nottawa, MI 49075
616-467-7185

Huffaker Engineering
1290 Holm Rd.
Petaluma, CA 94952

King & Queen Mufflers
Box 432
Plumsteadville, PA 18949

Stainless Steel Exhaust
 Center
378 N. Star Route
Corrales, NM 87048

Stebro
10 Leach St.
Massena, NY 13662

INSTRUMENTS, FACIA PANEL
Nisonger Corp.
P.O. Box 748
35 Bartels Pl.
New Rochelle, NY 10801

Rene Rufenacht
Gibelstrasse 39
CH-2540
Grenchen, Switzerland

Craig Seabrook
Whitworth Shop
14444 Watt Rd.
Novelty, OH 44072
216-338-5950

John Marks
Vintage Restoration
The Old Bakery
Windmill St.
Tunbridge Wells
Kent, England
Tunbridge Wells (0892) 25899

Stewart-Warner Corp.
Consumer Products
1826 Diversey Parkway
Chicago, IL 60614

INSURANCE

J. C. Taylor, Inc.
8701 W. Chester Ave.
Upper Darby, PA 19082
215-853-1300

Classic Insurance Agency
639 Lindberg Way N.E.
Atlanta, GA 30324
404-262-2264

Condon & Skelly
Antique Motor Car Insurance
P.O. Drawer A
Willingboro, NY 08046
609-871-1212

LITERATURE

Classic Motorbooks
P.O. Box 1
Osceola, WI 54020
715-294-3345

Connoisseur Carbooks
28 Devonshire Rd.
Chiswick, London
W4 2HD England

M.G. International
P.O. 2332
Springfield, MA 01101

Lawrence Mishou
1036 Whitman St.
Hanson, MA 02341
617-447-2662
(manuals)

METAL STRIPPERS

East Coast Metal Strippers
310-312 W. Main St.
Norristown, PA 19401
215-277-7538

Redi-Strip of PA
Jerry Fisher
Moor Ind. Park
1729 PA Ave.
Monaca, PA 15601
412-723-5535

MODELS, MINIATURES, TOYS

Miniature Toys, Inc.
Westboro, MA 01581

Richardis' Auto Models
P.O. Box 8
Parsippany, NJ 07054

Samuel A. Sheilds, Jr.
484 Lynn Dr.
Cayahoga Falls, OH 44221
216-928-9802

Sinclair's Auto Miniatures
3831 W. 12th St.
Erie, PA 16505

Tamara
P.O. Box 545
Warwick, RI 02887

The Little Toy Maker
David Hughes
123 Dartmoor
San Antonio, TX 78227
512-675-0094

Anthony Sciolto
R.R. 4
Box 209
Brandy Brook Rd.
N. Scituate, RI 02857
401-647-3392
(M.G. knobs)

Tecar Restorations
1098 Norris Lake Dr.
Lithonia, GA 30058
(M.G. mailbox name plates)

Brass & Silver, Ltd.
18019 Almond Rd.
Castro Valley, CA 94546

Dastal Printing Co.
1210 E. 286th St.
Cleveland, OH 44132
216-431-4161
(decals, stationery)

Kimble Engineering, Ltd.
33 Highfield Rd.
Hall Green, Birmingham B28 OEV
England

Pulfer & Williams
Robbins Rd. RFOL
Rindge, NH 03461
603-899-5659
(emblems, jewelry)

Register Regalia (TSO)
Dorothy Boiteau #57
92 Bowles Park
Springfield, MA 01104
413-737-8611

PARTS, CARS, FULL-LINE
SUPPLIERS

Abingdon Spares, Ltd.
P.O. Box 37, South St.
Walpole, NH 03608
603-756-4768

Auto Import Ass., Inc.
7813 NW 72nd Ave.
Medley, FL 33166

Bap/Geon
Toll Free 800-421-1425
call for nearest address

Beer of Houghton
Houghton, Huntington
PE172BD England

Beugler Strippers
P.O. Box 29068-C
Los Angeles, CA 90029

British Auto Parts
Excelsior Motors
2350 N. Damen Ave.
Chicago, IL 60647
312-252-6809

British Sports Car Parts
512 Boston Post Rd.
Darien, CT 06820
203-655-8731

Stan Brown
Woodland Rd.
Hampton, NH 02842

Champion Spark Plug Co.
Toledo, OH 43661
(consumer information)

C.K. Spares Company, Ltd.
St. Ives Rd.
Houghton
Huntington, England

Clover Machine Works
P.O. Box 3121
San Jose, CA 95156

D.J. Sports Cars
Swains Factory, Crane Mead
Ware, Hertfordshire,
Ware 5431, England

Edge Machine Co.
8403 Allport
Santa Fe Springs, CA 90670
213-945-3419

English Car Spares, Ltd.
1238 Fernwood Circle NE
Atlanta, GA 30319
404-233-1917

Foreign Autopart
1205 U.S. Rt. 1
P.O. Box AUTO
Sharon, MA 02067

G.K. Motors
Rear of 9, Old Highway
Rye Park
Hoddesdon, Hertfordshire
England

Jaguar Rover Triumph, Inc.
600 Willow Tree Rd.
Leonia, NJ 07605
(consumer information)
201-461-7300

J.C. Whitney & Co.
1900-24 So. State St.
P.O. Box 8410
Chicago, IL 60680

Joseph Lucas North America, Inc.
30 Van Nostrand Ave.
Englewood, NJ 07631
(consumer information)

Kimble Engineering
33 Highfield Rd.
Birmingham, England

M & G Vintage Auto
154 Chestnut St.
Ridgewood, NJ 07450
Toll Free 800-631-8991

Moss Motors, Ltd.
P.O. Box "MG"
7200 Hollister Ave.
Goleta, CA 93017
Toll Free 800-235-6954

NTG Motor Services, Ltd.
21 St. Margarets Green
Ipswich IP4 2BN
England

Octagon Sports Cars, Ltd.
19-21 Grosvernor Park Rd.
London E17 9PD England

Ped-Al-Loc
P.O. Box 17107
Pittsburgh, PA 15235

Penn Ball Bearing Co.
3511 N. American St.
Philadelphia, PA 19140

The Pre-War MG Parts Center
1a Albany Rd., Chislehurst
Kent, England
01-467-7788

P.S. Russell
c/o Peets Lane
Churchtown
Southport
Merseyside PR9 7PP
England

Sports and Vintage Motors Ltd.
Upper Battlefield
Shrewsbury SY4 3DB
England

Start Your Engines
P.O. Box TR&MG
Beltsville, MD 20705

Time Machines, Inc.
13 Neptune Ave.
Brooklyn, NY 11237
(silicone brake fluid)

Tioga Stainless
Water A. Grove
6 Deborah Dr.
Apalachin, NY 13732
607-625-4425
(nuts, bolts, pins, etc.)

Ernie Toth
8153 Cloverridge Rd.
Chagrin Falls, OH 44022
216-338-3565
(silicone brake fluid)

Toulmin Motors (1962), Ltd.
103 Windmill Rd.
Brentford, Middlesex
England
01-560 1722/2228

University Motors, Ltd.
614 Eastern Ave. SE
Grand Rapids, MI 49503
616-245-2141

Vintage Specialists
P.O. Box 70
Massapequa Park, NY 11762
516-541-0075

SEAT COVERS
Automotive Alliance
(Shear Comfort)
3527 Madera St.
P.O. Box 565
Santa Ynez, CA 93460
805-688-8808

CPR International
109 Second St.
Sausalito, CA 94065

Malare Trading Co.
1059 Traymore Blvd.
Island Park, NY 11558

SHOCK ABSORBER REBUILDERS
Novus Box 17985
Irvine, CA 92713
213-774-2761

SPOKE WHEEL REBUILDERS
Wheel Repair Service of
  New England
317 Southbridge St.
Auburn, MA 01501
617-799-6551

Wheels
W. London Repair Company, Ltd.
5 Lancaster Rd.
Wimbledon S.W., 19 England

TOOLS
Tom Lecklider
12 Pynchon Paddochs
Wrights Green
Little Mallingbury
Bishop's Stortford Herts
OM22 7RJ England
(Whitworth socket sets)

ETC
1948 S. La Cienega Blvd.
Los Angeles, CA 90034
Toll Free 800-421-0915
(air-powered tools)

TRIM, PAINT, UPHOLSTERY
Paul Beck
Happisburgh
Norwich, Norfolk
NR12 ORX England

George S. Cihochi
36 Carol St.
Enfield, CO 06082
203-745-2352

The Clausen Co.
1055 King George Rd.
P.O. Drawer 140
Fords, NJ 08863

Bill Hirsch
396 Littleton Ave.
Newark, NJ 07103
201-243-2858

Torgs
423 State St.
Santa Barbara, CA 93101

CLUBS

AMERICAN MGB ASSOCIATION
Attn: Club Secretary
P.O. Box 11401
Chicago, IL 60611

American "MGC" Register
Tom Boscarino, chairman
12 Charles St.
Islip Terrace, NY 11752

CANADIAN CLASSIC MG CLUB
H. Lunner
6491 Aperling Ave.
Burnaby, B.C.
V5E 2V3 Canada

MG OWNERS CLUB
13 Church End
Over
Cambridgeshire CB4 5NH England

MGA TWIN CAM REGISTRY
P.O. Box 1058
Anderson, Indiana 46015

MGA TWIN CAM REGISTRY
Jim Treat
2451 Stage Coach Tr. S.
Afton, MN 55001

The New England MGT
 Register, Ltd.
Drawer 220
Oneonta, New York 13820

North American MGA Register
5 Miller Fall Ct.
Derwood, Maryland 20855

THE M.G. CAR CLUB LIMITED
67 Wide Bargate
Boston, Lincs. PE21 5LE England

RECOMMENDED READING

Books

Allison, Mike. *The Magic of MG,* London: Dalton Watson, Ltd., 1972.

Christy, John, and Karl Ludvigsen. *The Complete MG Guide: Model by Model.* Blue Ridge Summit, Pennsylvania: Tab Books, 1980.

Knudson, Richard L. *MG International,* "ADO 23: The B Goes On." London: Motor Racing Publications, Ltd., 1977.

_____ . *M.G.: The Sports Car America Loved First.* Savannah, Georgia: Motorcars Unlimited, 1973.

_____ . *The T Series M.G.* Savannah, Georgia: Motorcars Unlimited, 1975.

_____ , and Francis Old. *The T Series Handbook.* Springfield, Massachusetts: The New England M.G. T Register, Ltd., 1981.

McComb, F. Wilson. *MG by McComb.* London: Osprey Publishing Ltd., 1978.

Robson, Graham. *The MGA, MGB, and MGC: A Collector's Guide.* London: Motor Racing Publications, Ltd., 1978.

Vitrikas, Robert P. *MGA: A History and Restoration Guide.* Tucson, Arizona: Aztec Corporation, 1980.

Periodicals

Automobile Quarterly
245 W. Main St.
Kutztown, PA 19530

Autoweek
965 E. Jefferson
Detroit, MI 48207

Car Collector & Car Classics
P.O. Box 171
Mount Morris, IL 61054

Cars & Parts
P.O. Box 482
Sidney, OH 45367

Car and Driver
One Park Ave.
New York, NY 10016

Hemmings Motor News
Box 100
Bennington, VT 05201

M.G. Magazine
2 Spencer Place
Scarsdale, NY 10583

Motor Trend
Petersen Publishing Co.
8490 Sunset Blvd.
Los Angeles, CA 90069

Old Cars
Iola, WI 54945

Road & Track
CBS Publications
1515 Broadway
New York, NY 10036

Special-Interest Autos
Dept. 205
Box 196
Bennington, VT 05201

Thoroughbred & Classic Cars
1 PC Business Press Ltd.
204 E. 42 St.
New York, NY 10017

Vintage Racer
P.O. Box 30628
Santa Barbara, CA 93105